THE ESSENTIAL FUNDING [...] [...]NEURS

THE
INVESTMENT
HANDBOOK

DAVID BATEMAN

Legend Press Ltd, 107-111 Fleet Street, London, EC4A 2AB
info@legend-paperbooks.co.uk | www.legendpress.co.uk

Print ISBN 9781787197909
Ebook ISBN 9781787197893
Set in Times. Printing managed by Jellyfish Solutions Ltd
Cover design by Simon Levy | www.simonlevyassociates.co.uk

THE INVESTMENT HANDBOOK

THE ESSENTIAL FUNDING GUIDE FOR ENTREPRENEURS

CONTENTS

Foreword   5
Thomas Hellman, Professor of Entrepreneurship and
Innovation, Said Business School, University of Oxford

Introduction   7
The Editor

PART ONE – PREPARING TO APPROACH AND   9
MEET INVESTORS

1.1 What Investors Want in Return   11
Jonathan Reuvid

1.2 Common Mistakes – an Investor's View   19
Eileen Modral, Investment Manager, OION

1.3 Valuing Your Business   25
Eileen Modral, Investment Manager, OION

PART TWO – DIRECTORY OF INVESTORS   31

2.1 **How to Use the Directory**   33
     Jonathan Reuvid

2.2 **UK Venture Capital Investors**   35

2.3 **UK Angel Networks**   65

2.4 **US Venture Capital Investors**   95

2.5 **US Angel Networks**   143

2.6 **Rest of World Capital Investors**   178

2.7 **Rest of World Angel Networks**   198

PART THREE – DOWN THE ROAD   207

3.1 **What to Do When You Don't Get Funding**   209
     David Bateman and Jonathan Reuvid

3.2 **Endgame**   216
     David Bateman

FOREWORD

In the role of Professor of Entrepreneurship at Oxford University I see many students who aspire to become successful entrepreneurs. Indeed, I even see a select few go on to achieve that goal, creating innovative and exciting businesses.

In my experience this process of launching a new enterprise can be both inspiring and thrilling, yet it is a hard path, at many times challenging, and requires dedication and persistence.

Indeed, one of the early challenges that an aspiring entrepreneur must overcome is raising capital in order to kick-start or grow their business. And despite being a process that almost all entrepreneurs and business owners must go through, it still strikes me as something of a 'random walk' at times, with few clear signposts as to where to go and who to talk to.

Starting out with personal contacts and introductions seems to be the norm for an entrepreneur who is looking for investment. This is usually combined with personal efforts at collating a 'hit list' of potential investors from various scattered resources across the Internet. But although this process is a well-trodden path by many entrepreneurs before, all too often it ends up as an inefficient and inconsistent approach from one business owner to another.

This book, along with the accompanying online data, consolidates the material that every entrepreneur needs when they are looking to raise capital. Having all of this information in a single publication provides an invaluable resource for you as an entrepreneur or business owner; it provides you with immediate information and contact details for access to many of the world's leading business investors.

The material also provides you with valuable information about an investor's preferred sectors that they allocate money to, along with details about their typical size of investment. This allows you to drill down to a more relevant target audience, and be far more efficient in your search for capital.

Accompanying the specific investor information and data, you will also find chapters that give insight as to how best to approach investors, what they look for and common pitfalls to avoid.

In summary, this resource consolidates so much valuable information that it has the potential to create incredible savings for one of your most valuable commodities as an entrepreneur – your time!

As a final word, raising capital for a new business can be a daunting process, but with the right approach, attitude and resources, it can be a far more straightforward and rewarding experience than you might at first expect. With this in mind, I thoroughly recommend this resource to help you along your way and I wish you the very best of luck and success with your venture.

Thomas Hellmann, Professor of Entrepreneurship and Innovation
Said Business School, University of Oxford

INTRODUCTION

This book from David Bateman is the perfect companion title to his widely acclaimed *Business Plans That Get Investment*, which equips entrepreneurs with the essential tools for attracting investors' attention. This Investment Handbook leads the reader through the process of selecting the most likely sources of funding from the directory of angel networks and venture capital funds listed in the book which are identified with their sector of interest.

Along the way entrepreneurs are schooled in what investors look for in return for their investments, the common mistakes made in engaging and negotiating with potential investors and valuing your business realistically. Contributions from Eileen Modral, Investment Network Manager of Oxford Investment Opportunity Network provide authoritative, experience-based insight on these topics and investor mindsets. In further chapters, David Bateman offers practical advice on what to do if you fail to get funding and on the endgame alternatives attractive to external investors who do invest.

Legend Business Books is delighted to be continuing its association with David with this new Guide. Our sincere thanks also to Eileen and to Thomas Hellman, Professor of Entrepreneurship and Innovation, Said Business School, University of Oxford, for his Foreword.

Jonathan Reuvid, Editor

PART ONE

PREPARING TO APPROACH
AND MEET INVESTORS

1.1

WHAT INVESTORS WANT IN RETURN

Jonathan Reuvid

Careful study of investors' profiles and the businesses in which they have invested recently will give you a clear idea of the niche areas to which they are attracted. It will also indicate the scale and nature of funds they commit to individual enterprises and the equity participation they are looking for. All investors are risk averse to the unfamiliar and if your venture falls outside their broader fields of interest and experience, it is unlikely that you will attract attention.

However, before attempting to identify specific investor targets it is important that you understand the common requirements and preferences that all investors are likely to have so that you may structure your investment proposal and subsequently pitch accordingly. They fall under the following broad categories:

- Presentation and initial contact
- Pitch and preliminary discussion
- Growth and scalability of business

- Management capability
- Detailed Business Plans
- Risk / reward assessment

Only when the investor is satisfied on all six counts will more detailed discussion take place leading to negotiation of terms and ultimately a Term Sheet to be approved by all parties which will form the basis for detailed documentation and due diligence.

Before discussing the likely structure of any investment deal that may be on offer, let's review in turn each of the six requirements.

PRESENTATION

Your first objective is simply to attract investors' attention sufficiently so that you are invited to attend a meeting to make your pitch and hold a preliminary discussion. The most effective way to make your approach is an email to the potential investors you have selected enclosing a PDF of your headline Business Plan. Be sure to follow the seasoned advice in David Bateman's book *Business Plans that Get Investment*; the nub of his advice on constructing your plan is to follow the familiar KISS dictum: "keep it simple, stupid".

As David emphasises, most professional investors receive up to 100 approaches with Business Plans every week and most of these end up in the bin. To gain attention your Plan needs to be clear and concise, delivering its message and your core proposition within the first five minutes of reading which is probably all the time that an investor will give to their first scan. A confused message with a jumble of secondary detail and a lack of structure, however well written, will be fatal to further reading.

The structure which David advocates is a package of no more than 14 pages arranged and titled as follows:

1. **Executive Summary** – An overview of what is to come.
2. **Opportunity** – What problem or gap in the market your business addresses.
3. **Background** – The product your business makes or the service it offers.
4. **USP** – The Unique Selling Pont (USP) that makes your business special and different from others.

5. **Progress** – The progress you have made in developing your business and its current position, including any successes to date.
6. **The Market** – The identity and characteristics of your customers.
7. **Route to Market** – How you plan to access and sell to your potential customers.
8. **Competition** – Who else does what you do or something similar.
9. **Management** – Who runs the business and what is their experience and knowledge of the sector.
10. **Business Model** – How the business makes money, explaining the manufacturing cost of the product , or provision of the service, through to the proceeds from actual sales.
11. **Financials** – Current and future sales, costs and profits.
12. **Investment** – How much investment you are asking for and what you plan to do with it.
13. **Exit** – How the investor will get their money back from their investment and generate an additional return.
14. **Conclusion** – A brief synopsis of the plan, similar to the Executive Summary but finishing on a 'high note' with the most favourable points.

For the structure of each page bullet points are recommended with no more than six bullet points on each page including the financials. A template is provided on the website www.businessplansthatgetinvestment.com to which purchasers of the book have access in PowerPoint landscape format as an exemplar for any Business Plan.

When writing your Business Plan, be aware of the criteria that investors who persist in reading beyond the first five minutes will apply. And here it may be helpful to differentiate between the three broad categories of equity investor, not rigidly compartmentalised, who are business angels, venture capitalists and private equity.

• All three often, though not always the case with private equity, start out with the general expectation that no more than 30% of their investments will be successful. Therefore, they look for high returns from those that prosper. In venture capital, the rule of thumb is that only 10% are winners.
• Most business angels and venture capitalists aim to exit their investments within three to four years. Larger equity funds may take a

longer view. However, take four years as the norm for the time period of your planning.

- Before clinching a deal you will need to demonstrate 'proof of concept': that your product or service has a market, is commercially viable and will make money.

Angel investors are usually businesspeople who have often started successful businesses which are the basis of their wealth and who favour early stage businesses. They may be keen to offer expertise and experience to the start-ups in which they invest. Individually their personal investment may be a little as £10,000 and is unlikely to exceed £100,000. They tend to hunt in packs through managed networks such as the Oxford Invenstment Opportunity Network (OION), which forms a new investment company each year in which individuals invest as a syndicate to take advantage of the government's Enterprise Investment Scheme (EIS) or Seed Enterprise Investment Scheme (SEIS) offering relief from Capital Gains Tax (CGT). There is a preference by such networks for innovative high-tech businesses. Early investment equity funding by angel consortia is most suitable for companies seeking from £75,000 to £250,000.

Venture capitalists are focused on companies that already have some track record. They are professionally managed investment companies in their own right and are probably more demanding than angel investor syndicates in terms of Business Plans and management team capabilities. They like to offer funding packages in excess of £250,000, which minimize their risk exposure by providing at least part of the investment in loans or most of it in preference shares with only a small proportion as unprotected ordinary share capital.

Private equity funds also encompass the larger investment companies that provide multi-million pound funding and sometimes involve themselves in supporting acquisitions and corporate rescues.

PITCH AND PRELIMINARY DISCUSSION

Your initial pitch was your Business Plan and, if it did its job successfully, it will elicit invitations to meet and discuss. But do not expect that responses will be unsolicited. Prepare yourself for telephone follow-ups after one week to all that have not sent "thank you but no thank you" replies to your email. Verbal follow-ups are of crucial importance.

At your first meeting with a prospective investor expect to be questioned closely on all elements of your Business Plan and prepare accordingly. Have back-up information available as hand-outs but use sparingly, only where there is demand for further detail. However, the face-to-face encounter has more dimensions than cross-examination of the Plan. This is the investor's first opportunity to appraise you personally and any members of your management team who attend with you. As well as satisfying the investor on your plans and your ability to carry them out, this is an opportunity to establish whether there is sufficient compatibility and the confidence to proceed further.

And the dialogue is a two-way street; it's your opportunity to establish a basis of sufficient trust in the investor team for you to feel comfortable in continuing to talk. Before meeting again or exchanging further information you may be asked to sign a mutual non-disclosure agreement (NDA) in order to protect sensitive information or intellectual property of both parties.

GROWTH AND SCALEABILITY OF BUSINESS

Growth can result from general growth of the market in which you operate or from your increasing penetration of the market as a result of your business's USP (Unique Selling Points). Investors will look for evidence of both.

"Scalability" is an attractive and often necessary condition for equity investment. This means that if your company operates in a market niche and has a Business Plan showing geometric growth rates its chances of securing investment are greatly enhanced.

MANAGEMENT CAPABILITY

Innovative brilliance, sound business strategy and thorough understanding of the market(s) in which you operate are all strong plus points in assessing management capability. However, they are not enough to convince experienced investors. You will also need to show that your management team has depth and has appropriate 'been there, done that' experience.

Young management teams have an advantage in terms of perceived energy and enthusiasm but you may need to add one or two older members, over 40, in supporting roles such as finance or, perhaps a non-executive Chair with an established reputation and connections. The executive management needs to be full-time without other work engagements. You also need to be aware that, from an investor's viewpoint, 'capability' includes financial commitment. The core management team will be expected to invest significant personal funds for their shareholdings. The terms of the deal may include the provision of loan capital to management for their investments, sometimes secured on their personal assets.

DETAILED BUSINESS PLANS

The financials in the Business Plan that you have sent are headline numbers, confined to revenue, gross profit, net profit and net margins over four years with notes highlighting margins and growth and, maybe, references to bank debt and directors' investment. As discussions progress you and your financial director will be required to provide much more detail in terms of revenue sources, variable costs, gross margins, overheads and cashflow forecasts incorporating all these elements

You need to have this information in your back pocket at the first meeting, but do not provide your spreadsheets until requested. You may find that more detail or projections for alternative scenarios are required.

RISK / REWARD ASSESSMENT

The degree to which an investor is risk averse will affect the decision to go forward and also the structure of any investment package that may be offered. The assessment of the risk/reward involved will be conditioned by past experience of investment in companies in the same or similar fields. The calculated investment return is a key determinant and each investor will have its own yardsticks for measuring the rate of return. An exceptionally high rate of return from an innovative product or service is not necessarily an added inducement; it may raise concerns that your market is vulnerable to new entrants and discounting.

Two of the most common measurement tools are EBITDA and IRR. EBITDA is the acronym for earnings before interest on debt, corporation tax, depreciation and amortisation and the more complex IRR for "internal rate of return". IRR, much favoured by private equity, is the calculated total return over the life of an investment in terms of cash received from dividends and interest plus the cash recovered on exit, net of tax and discounted by the time intervals before receipt (i.e. their present value), expressed as a percentage of the original investment. There are a number of variations on the calculation of IRR which can be found online and Excel has a function to calculate its own variation.

INVESTMENT PACKAGES

Most investors are looking for an interest in the ordinary share capital or equity of a target company of more than 25% but it is unlikely, except for angel syndicates, that any offer will take the form of a straightforward subscription for Ordinary Shares.

However risk tolerant an investor, they are likely to offer a package which includes either or both of a subscription for Preference Shares (which is another form of equity) and the provision of loan capital in the form of Loan Stock (i.e debt) with conversion rights into equity at the investor's time of choice. The initial investment may include only a relatively small element of ordinary shares with the major part offered in either Preference Shares or Loan Stock with conversion rights into ordinary shares attached. When exercised, they will bring the investor's equity holding up to and perhaps above the level with which you might feel comfortable. In the meantime, voting rights on Preference Shares or Loan Stock restrictions on further debt will give the investor a degree of financial control and limit the downside risk. Of course, both Loan Stock and Preference Shares come with interest charges which will impact profits and the availability of dividends on Ordinary Shares and you should consider carefully the implications of rolled up charges and penalties in the event that the company is unable to pay interest at the due dates.

Most investment packages also come with requirements that executive directors should enter into service agreements. The company may also be required to take out key person insurance, at least for the Chief Executive, providing cover in the event of disability or death during the period of service. As many investments are made to back the key individuals as well as the business, it will be vital for an investor that the key individuals are fully tied into the business and there is a contingency in place should they no longer be able to fulfil their roles.

1.2

COMMON MISTAKES TO BE AVOIDED WHEN RAISING INVESTMENT

Eileen Modral, Investment Manager, OION Ltd

INTRODUCTION

Raising investment is a serious part of any business and takes time and effort for both entrepreneur and investors, so preparation is essential. With so many interesting opportunities now in competition for investment it is far easier for any investor to walk away when problems arise. So avoiding simple errors at this stage can be the difference between getting a follow up meeting or not.

For the 24 plus years that Oxford Investment Opportunity Network Ltd has been supporting entrepreneurs and investors the early stage investment sector has evolved, not just through the advancement of technologies but in who, how and why investment happens. From crowdfunding that has enabled new models to evolve but also, as a result of the advancement of tax breaks under the Seed Enterprise Investment Scheme (SEIS) and the Enterprise Investment Scheme (EIS), the sector has flourished.

However, the fundamentals of investing have changed very little: the due diligence and the risk reward balance considered by investors are still basically the same, be they angels or VCs. The size of investment may differ but it takes as much time and money for an investor to make an investment of £5,000,000 as it does of £50,000.

What has also been consistent are the mistakes that entrepreneurs make when setting out and during fundraising. These are many and varied; so what has been set out below is a broad view around areas of timing and due diligence. It is not comprehensive or exhaustive but does cover the most common errors. These mistakes are often interlinked and also impact at the important stage of that first face to face meeting with an investor. Valuing your business is the subject of a further chapter.

Types of funding

There are only three basic funding types: Grant, Equity and Debt. There may be many variations on these three, but grants are usually for early stage companies looking to do research and development of a product to validate the market, building value in the business and reducing risk in preparation for equity investment. However, remember that grants also take time to submit and then deliver and, if it is not part of the core business for the company, then this can be a distraction. For the purposes of this chapter high-risk equity investment is the focus and a quick tour of the timing and due diligence process is set out below.

TIMING

Remember it is usually more difficult to attract funding when really needed; so always plan well ahead for what, when, how and why. The process usually takes longer and often the company under-estimates how much funding is required.

How to approach investors is important; with so many opportunities passing across an investor's desk how to get past that first email delete or submission archive is critical.

Providing information

Usually, it is not expected that an exhaustive Business Plan will be sent out on initial contact; a summary Business Plan as outlined elsewhere in this book is ideal. This should be accompanied by a brief introductory letter that outlines the business, the sector and the minimum funding amount required..

Never provide more than is requested by the investor, but always in a timely manner and in a form that is easily accessible. Sending a link to an obscure file share or a website for the investor to do their own research is not acceptable.

Early stage first-mover advantage-type companies will be expected to have initial sales that prove the market; so timing in funding is usually about full commercialisation and breaking even. Selling to individuals, other companies or distributors all have their own market expectations and risk. Therefore, timing with a three-year cashflow makes sense, or possibly four as David Bateman suggests in his Business Plan template, as after the first three years the advantage dissipates.

An early stage spin-out company from a university that has strong Intellectual Property to exploit will have a longer time to first sales. So timing with a five-year cashflow plan with assumptions provides more information than a very detailed sales forecast.

How much to ask for
Don't fit the funding to the investor; the funding should fit the needs of the company. Early stage companies where SEIS advanced assurance can be used to attract investors looking to take advantage of the tax break will often say they are raising £150,000 to £250,000 as this fits the level of SEIS. On further inspection it is often to cover research or development of a product for the next 4-6 months.

If a company really needs £500,000 to deliver on its Business Plan for the next 18 to 24 months, then that is the amount of funding the company should be raising and the expected timescale. It comes back to 'raising funding takes time and effort'; so ensuring a funding runway that takes risk out of the business makes more sense, as the next investment round should be at a higher valuation for the company and the investor.

DUE DILIGENCE

Due diligence is a central part of securing finance and not just for investors. The number of times investors have received an email that has either been copied to a list, without personal salutation or is completely inappropriate to their investment interest, are countless.

Entrepreneurs should be doing their own due diligence on the investors that they are contacting. Check out their investment level, sector, portfolio of companies, whether they are currently investing, with whom do they usually invest alongside, or do they invest alone? These are all simple basic questions that should be part of an entrepreneur's due diligence checklist.

Be aware that the investor sector is a small community; so always be honest. Saying that there are soft commitments from other VCs or angels is not a good move if there are not. Do not be evasive; if you do not have information or know the answer, then say so. Listen to what is being asked, then provide documents and information.

For early stage investors and VCs, due diligence is an important part of their business which involves a thorough examination of any business, product, financial records if relevant and how they fit in with the whole Business Plan. This is the way to validate information through these documents.

For early stage investors due diligence is an important justification for why they may invest their money. For VCs due diligence is key to providing validation and substance to the investors in their fund. It is part of the process of administering funds on behalf of others and provides checks and balances on assertions made by an entrepreneur and identifies key areas of risk.

Due diligence falls into broad categories. Most early stage investors will have only some area of expertise and that is one of the reasons why some investors syndicate. It is also why the people aspect is important both for the investor and the entrepreneur; a mutual respect and trust must be built.

For VCs each category will be undertaken by experts within that field. In addition to accounting and legal professionals there are organisations dedicated to providing commercial and technology-specific technical due diligence.

Preparation by the entrepreneur in providing the right documents and contacts is paramount. The type of document and information to be considered is often underestimated by the entrepreneur and that is a mistake that stops an investor in its tracks.

Financial due diligence
Historical, current and anticipated future financial performance of the company is reviewed in detail. For later stage companies the income and expenditure

should be fully and correctly recorded and be produced as statutory accounts. Financial due diligence also examines the quality of the financial information prepared for management purposes.

Early stage investments may not have a significant financial track record and that is why the cashflow is important along with the forecasts and assumptions of the company, all of which will be reviewed. But be prepared for the assumptions behind the numbers to be challenged. Salaries and overheads will also be scrutinised, particularly if a large part of the investment is for salaries. No investor would want entrepreneurs to worry about how they will live and eat but salaries at a sensible level for the stage of business will show a commitment to put funds back into the company alongside the investor.

Legal due diligence
The strength of the company's legal and contractual framework is reviewed. The review includes employment contracts, statutory documentation (e.g. incorporation documents, board minutes etc.), agreements with third parties (confidentiality, licensing, agency, terms of business etc.). The company is also investigated for potential litigation and the legal validity of any intellectual property is also assessed.

Some early stage companies with founder directors should be aware that they will still need an employment contract. Directors' loans and salaries will also be reviewed.

Technical due diligence
This is particularly relevant for innovative products and involves a critical evaluation of the product for its technical fitness and uniqueness or superiority over competing products.

The team and strategic partners will also be scrutinised to enable the investor to make a judgment as to whether they have the skill, experience and appetite to develop and improve the product effectively within its market, and within the both the physical and business environment.

Commercial due diligence
The future profitability of any product or service is significantly influenced by the market environment it enters so commercial due diligence investigates that market and its key drivers for value for the product or service. The principal areas of risk are investigated to form an opinion on whether the sales forecasts prepared by the company are realistically achievable.

The report will include an investigation into the market in terms of current, historic and anticipated future growth trends. The impact of competition is also considered in terms of both existing competition and the potential for new players to enter the market. The regulatory environment may also be taken into consideration, e.g. environmental legislation and its impact on the clean/green technology market.

Building a new market as a first mover is far riskier than entering a rising market. If sales, advanced orders or intent to buy are mentioned then contact the client to let them know they they may be contacted or have the company write a brief 'Letter of Intent' that provides evidence of potential sales.

Having produced an enticing Business Plan and succeeded in having a Term Sheet agreed with investors, it would be great pity to then trip up at the due diligence stage so preparation and being as comprehensive as possible are key. Additionally, what is provided during due diligence can be considered legally disclosed, which is very important when it comes to the personal warranties entrepreneurs will need to sign confirming they provided the investors with all relevant information prior to their investment.

1.3

VALUING YOUR BUSINESS

Eileen Modral, Investment Manager, OION Ltd

Knowing how to value a company – especially in a start-up or fast-growing business – is extremely difficult and at this stage it is more of an art than a science.

There is a lot of support out there with numerous source documents and clever spreadsheets that at the click of a button will demonstrate your value. Unfortunately, early stage companies are probably too early stage to make those calculations meaningful; so realistically it will be down to a negotiation between the entrepreneur and investors.

VALUING REALISTICALLY

It is important therefore to set expectations at a reasonable level before discussing the details of an investment with an investor and one of the biggest mistakes a company makes is to value unrealistically.

Most investors see a great many deals and active investors recognise how long it can take to put together a good deal. If an investor is interested and has in mind that they would be willing to invest to get 20 % of the company, with a valuation that will mean they will get only 1% of the company, both parties' views are so far apart that negotiation seems pointless and the investor will simply walk away.

If a company overvalues itself, say at £5 million for a pre-revenue, high risk technology company that has an unproven commercial management team etc., then investors will simply not take the investment seriously.

At an angel round for a pre-revenue company in a high-growth market with a proven management team the chances are valuation expectation by the investor would be at around £500,000 - £1,000,000. It is reasonable to expect someone who puts in £100,000 at this stage to get at least 10 - 20% of your company. As said before, an art rather than science.

NEGOTIATING A VALUE

Negotiation is the key to a decent valuation; so come to the table in the strongest possible position from a commercial perspective.

If desperate for money, a company's valuation will be lower; so start the process with some cash in the bank if possible to survive a long negotiation period. Always assume it will take at least six months to raise investment.

There is nothing more convincing to an investor than to see that a company has attracted other experienced people to the business (either as investors, advisors, board members, mentors etc). As a start-up business building a team is essential and the members do not all need to be employees.

Back reasoning up with examples from elsewhere – it does no harm to work out a discounted terminal value or to find similar examples of companies that have successfully floated. Investors may not take those assumptions particularly seriously but they do strengthen the case.

Valuation is by no means one-sided. If the investor is 'just the money' then the company's valuation can be higher than if an investor is adding extra non-financial support (e.g. contacts, credibility, Board position etc.). Look for the right investor at the right time for the business.

When a company is too early stage to make any of the normal valuation methods work (e.g. multiples of revenue, discounted cashflows etc), then it normally goes back to a gut feeling about what will motivate both sides.

Remember to allow for future rounds of investment (and therefore dilution) in your thinking as well as setting aside an option pool. Don't opt for money 'at any price', as a lower valuation with the right investor is better than having to deal with disgruntled investors when expectations are not achieved.

Most investors are keen to come to a fair deal to ensure that motivation remains and both sides have the potential to make a significant return. If the balance is not right in either direction the company is likely to fail.

Exits are important but ensure there is an understanding of the timeframe for the different investors. SEIS investors must hold shares for a minimum of three years. VCs are expecting to make high returns and multiple staged investments, but their fund will usually have an expected and published timescale for investing and close.

FURTHER CONSIDERATIONS

As a final reminder of common mistakes made by entrepreneurs when it comes to valuation, it is important to remember that the development of new businesses based upon innovative products and services usually requires a significant amount of funding to get off the ground. Eliminating simple errors when starting out on the process and building credibility along the way will help when that initial interest turns into a first meeting with an investor.

The broader story around these points is having a strong narrative on what is the problem being solved and whether there is anyone else who is trying to solve it:

- Will development take so long that there is a risk new entrants to the marketplace could make the product redundant?
- Is the business a must-have or nice-to-have solution? Be sure what the unique sales proposition (USP) is and, most importantly, be able to explain it clearly and concisely. Talk to potential clients and get their backing for assumptions.
- Know the market, what is the addressable size or sector of that market and don't exaggerate. Be sensible in describing the size of the potential market. Factor in how easy it will be to reach potential customers and who is likely to be a first customer. Many businesses start up full of confidence and never think realistically about the scale of the market they are seeking to penetrate. Remember, a start-up company is small; so target the right market and the right customers first. Don't waste time, energy and money trying to reach everyone.
- Does the business idea or product 'disrupt' the market, in which case does the market want to be disrupted? Changing a sector is near impossible; so does the product complement the existing market, can it be retro-fitted, or used alongside existing technology or products?
- Is the business up in a rising market, or on the downward slope of a saturated market? Technology trends are much faster than they used to be.

Not all competitors are rivals, so know the difference. There may be potential collaborators out there, so identify the right ones early, build the relationship, as they may provide the next stage of funding or exit for early investors.

Prepare yourself to assess the following issues:

- What is the business model?
- Who is going to pay for your product and how will you make money?
- Where and who will be the first sale? What is the pipeline? As a founder can you sell your product or service, will you be the one making the first sales? If not, make sure you have the right people around you to sell the business products.
- Raising funding and securing investment can be a full-time job, so who will run the business while you are raising the funding? Picking the right team is very important.
- Are there key people on your Board that the sector will recognise? In a small business, ensure everyone shares the same aims and objectives, have an appropriate spread of skills and that they all get along with one another

Raise only what funding is needed, but ensure it is enough to reach milestones to the next stage funding. Allow for at least an 18-24 months horizon. Work out cash flow and remember everything takes twice as long, or costs twice as much as anticipated – whether it be raising funding, making that first sale, or waiting for the first invoice to be paid. Use grants to your advantage and where it fits with the business plan. Do not become a company that chases grants and forgets its real path to profitability.

Can an investor bring more than just money? Most importantly, ensure there are people around the business who have done it all before and can offer invaluable advice and support. Remember too that there are other support services needed as a business develops – no one is an expert in everything and everyone needs a network of experts to draw on items such as Intellectual Property, finance, law, marketing, PR, and HR.

HORSES FOR COURSES

The equity gap has been described as an amount between £100,000 and £2m that businesses find the most difficult to raise equity finance for.

At the start of a business the entrepreneur will raise funding through friends, family and contacts. The Business Angel investor provides that vital investment that will take a business through proof of concept funding to revenue generation. At the later stage Venture Capital investment provides expansion and pre-IPO funding.

Finally, here's an approximate guide to help you assess where your valuation is relative to the stage of growth of your business:

Company Stage	Typical Investment	Status	Source
Seed Capital (1st Round)	Up to £50K	Great idea. Proof of Principle/ Concept. Need finance for additional research or to produce a prototype	Ideas are too early for investment. Grants, awards special interest groups, friends, family and contact. Could be bank debt
Start-Up (1st Round or 2nd Round)	Up to £500K	Researched market & established prototype. Not generated sales yet .Finance needed for working capital ie. Initial marketing, salaries, product testing	Some early stage funding through VC, angels or corporate venturing in specific sectors
Early Stage (2nd Round)	£50K to £750K	Completed product & generating sales. Finance needed for marketing & operations to make business take off	Most equity funding options, grants or bank debt
Expansion Stage (2nd Round or 3rd Round)	£100K Upwards (£2M+ VC Funding)	Established business & generating profit. Finance needed for developing new products or exploring new markets	Most equity funding sources.

Source: Oxford Innovation Limited

Whatever investor you approach, bear in mind the following essentials:

1. It is often difficult to attract funding when a company really needs it.
2. Think ahead and plan to fundraise well in advance.
3. Take advice from people who have done it for similar businesses.
4. Work out exactly how much and what sort of funding you will require.
5. Plan whom it is appropriate to approach.
6. Provide them with the information they are looking for, in the format they want
7. Communicate effectively and honestly.
8. Summarise the objectives for the business to communicate them succinctly and with impact and conviction.
9. Ensure a company's objectives have a commercial focus.
10. Sell the business, not the product

PART TWO

DIRECTORY OF INVESTORS

2.1

HOW TO USE THE DIRECTORY

Jonathan Reuvid

The directory is arranged in six sections for ease of use:

- UK Venture Capital Investors
- UK Angel Networks
- US Venture Capital Networks
- US Angel Networks
- Rest of World Venture Capital Investors
- Rest of World Angel Networks

PRIMARY SELECTION

Your first selection choice therefore is to decide which section to visit first according to the maturity of your business and the amount of funding you are looking for. Part One of the book will help you to decide which are most appropriate. If you are a UK business, you will look first at the two lists of investors located in the UK, but bear in mind that if you are an IT business you could attract attention from investors specialising in that sector located in the USA or Europe.

Location

The investors in each of the directory lists are arranged by name in alphabetical order with their location immediately below, followed by the currency in which they invest and the value of their funds.

Targeting

The countries to which their investments are targeted are shown in column 5.

SECONDARY SELECTION CRITERIA

Industry sectors

The sectors of interest to each investor are next identified under the heading "Bio". You are unlikely to tempt investors into activities other than their preferred range.

Investment value

In most cases investors then indicate the minimum and maximum amounts that they choose to invest in a single project. Examples of companies in which they have invested (their "Portfolios") are sometimes given which is helpful if no range of investment value has been identified.

Maturity

Most investors also declare the preferred maturity of the businesses they support, classified as Seed, Start-up, Early or Mid-Stage and Late Stage with "Growth" specified in some cases.

This information should enable you to extract short lists of the most promising potential investors for your business.

COMMUNICATIONS

The final data listed for each entry are the investor's website address, contact email and, in many cases, contact telephone number.

2.2

UK VENTURE CAPITAL INVESTORS

3i
Location: London, Europe, Asia, North America
Currency: GBP
Size: 519m
Targeting: Northern Europe and Northern America
Bio: Specialist investors in business services, consumer and industrials.
Investment: 100m - 500m
Stage: Late Stage
Website: www.3i.com
Contact tel: +44 2079753131

Adam Street Partners
Location: Beijing, Chicago, London,Menlo Park, Singapore, Tokyo
Currency: USD
Size: 27bn
Targeting: Worldwide
Bio: Invest in rapidly growing, category-leading venture and growth companies across multiple stages, targeting software, mobile, big data, financial technology (fintech), security and healthcare.
Investment: 5m - 25m

Portfolio: BrightRoll, Couchbase, Donuts +
Stage: Late Stage
Website: www.adamsstreetpartners.com

Accelerator Group, The
Location: London
Targeting: US, Europe
Bio: Focus on the Internet services, e-commerce and multi-channel retail sectors.
Stage: Early Stage
Website: www.acceleration-group.com

Add Partners
Location: London
Currency: EUR
Targeting: Europe
Bio: Invest in Europe's most promising and ambitious IT and communications businesses.
Investment: 500k - 5m
Stage: Early & Mid Stage
Website: www.addpartners.net
Contact email: info@addpartners.net
Contact tel: +44 7530559100

Adfisco
Location: London
Targeting: UK, Europe, Middle East
Bio: Aim to back innovative financial services businesses, emerging from the disruptions in the financial sector. Fintech and data.
Portfolio: Funding Circle, Small World, Prodigy +
Stage: Early Stage & Growth
Website: www.adfisco.com
Contact email: enquiries@adfisco.com
Contact tel: +44 2079376690

Advent Venture Partners
Location: London
Currency: USD
Size: 266m
Targeting: UK, Europe, USA

Bio: Target tech & life science businesses in Europe.
Portfolio: DailyMotion, Qype +
Stage: Late Stage
Website: www.adventventures.com
Contact email: info@adventventures.com
Contact tel: +44 2079322100

Albion Ventures
Location: London
Currency: GBP
Size: 230m
Targeting: UK
Bio: The group boasts an investment portfolio of over 90 companies, including everything from tech-centric start-ups to service and asset-based companies.
Investment: 1 - 10m
Portfolio: Academia, Blackbay, Proveca +
Stage: Late Stage
Website: www.albion-ventures.co.uk
Contact email: info@albion-ventures.co.uk
Contact tel: +44 2076011850

Alchemy Partners
Location: London
Currency: GBP
Size: 1.5bn
Targeting: Europe
Bio: Focus on private equity and distressed investing.
Stage: Late Stage
Website: www.alchemypartners.co.uk
Contact email: info@alchemypartners.com
Contact tel: +44 2072409596

Allegro Capital
Location: London
Currency: USD
Size: 50m
Targeting: Worldwide - but focus on London based firms
Bio: Focusses on fashion, retail and consumer space.

Stage: Early & Mid Stage
Website: www.allegro-capital.com
Contact email: info@allegro-capital.com

Altitude Partners
Location: Southampton
Currency: USD
Size: 11m
Targeting: UK
Bio: Limited focus on businesses thriving in Southern England. They don't discriminate against any particular sector, but don't invest in start-up business or small management buy-ins.
Investment: 3m
Portfolio: Chameleon Worldwide Travel, The Care Division, Gradwell.
Stage: Late Stage
Website: www.altitudepartners.co.uk
Contact email: enquiries1@altitudepartners.co.uk
Contact tel: +44 2380002030

Amadeus Capital Partners
Location: London
Currency: USD
Size: 443m
Targeting: Europe, UK
Bio: They invest in all forms of technology, including healthcare, resource efficiency and clean-tech. All levels from seed, to venture buyout and everything in between.
Portfolio: Celltick, Bellco, GreenRoad +
Stage: Late Stage
Website: www.amadeuscapital.com
Contact tel: +44 2070246900

Anthemis Group
Location: London
Targeting: Worldwide
Bio: Invests in fintech sectors, including retail and corporate banking, consumer finance, payments, insurance and risk management and more.
Portfolio: Betterment, eShares, Seedcamp +

Stage: Early & Mid Stage
Website: www.anthemis.com
Contact tel: +44 2036530100

Ariadne Capital

Location: London
Currency: USD
Size: 7m
Targeting: UK
Bio: Targeting B2B tech start-ups focused on industries like health, transportation and financial services.
Investment: 250k - 1m
Portfolio: Quill, Clickslide +
Stage: Early & Mid Stage
Website: www.ariadnecapital.com
Contact email: newops@ariadnecapital.com
Contact tel: +44 2030211641

Arts Alliance

Location: London
Targeting: Europe
Bio: Investing in film, online advertising and online marketing.
Portfolio: Brainient, Shazam, Kebony, Graze +
Stage: Late Stage
Website: www.artsalliance.co.uk
Contact tel: +44 2073617720

Atomico

Location: London, Sao Paolo, Beijing, Tokyo, Istanbul, Cayman Islands
Currency: USD
Size: 641m
Targeting: Europe, USA, Asia
Bio: Atomico is a growth stage international investment firm, founded by the co-founder of Skype. Focuses exclusively on tech.
Portfolio: Last.fm, Skype, Rovio +
Stage: Seed, early stage and later stage venture as well as private equity investors
Website: www.atomico.com
Contact email: contact@atomico.com

Augmentum Capital
Location: London
Currency: USD
Size: 71m
Targeting: UK, Europe
Bio: Typically back early and late stage ventures, but want to stay with the business for as long as possible.
Investment: 3 - 20m
Portfolio: Borro, Zopa, Bullion Vault +
Stage: Late Stage
Website: www.augmentumcapital.com
Contact email: info@augmentumcapital.com
Contact tel: +44 2075141998

Balderton Capital
Location: London
Currency: USD
Size: 2bn
Targeting: Europe
Bio: Focusses mainly on e-commerce, consumer internet and software.
Investment: 100k – 20m
Portfolio: Betfair, Bebo, Citymapper, Wonga, Lovefilm +
Stage: Late Stage
Website: www.balderton.com
Contact tel: +44 2070166800

Ballpark Ventures
Location: London
Targeting: UK
Bio: Primarily focus on media, retail and technology.
Portfolio: Borro, Zopa, Bullion Vault +
Stage: Early & Mid Stage
Website: www.ballparkventures.com
Contact email: info@ballparkventures.com

Barclays & TechStars Accelerator
Location: London, New York, Cape Town, Tel Aviv
Targeting: Worldwide

Bio: Fintech focused
Investment: 120k
Website: www.barclaysaccelerator.com
Contact email: greg.rogers@techstars.com

Beacon Capital
Location: London
Currency: USD
Size: 300m
Bio: B2B, SaaS-based business models.
Investment: 200k - 2m
Portfolio: Adbrain, Azimo, Flypay, MOVE Guides, Seedrs, Shopa
Stage: Early & Mid Stage
Website: www.beaconcapital.co.uk

Big Issue Invest
Location: London
Currency: GBP
Size: 30m
Targeting: UK
Bio: One of the UK's leading providers of finance to social enterprises, community organisations, charities and businesses that are socially driven.
Investment: 50k - 1.5m
Stage: Early & Mid Stage
Website: www.bigissueinvest.com
Contact email: enquiries@bigissueinvest.com
Contact tel: +44 2075263440

Bridges Ventures
Location: London
Currency: USD
Size: 900m
Targeting: Not Specified
Bio: They run 3 separate funds, one for property, one for social enterprises and another for sustainable growth.
Investment: 15m
Stage: Late Stage

Website: www.bridgesfundmanagement.com
Contact email: info@bridgesventures.com
Contact tel: +44 2037808000

Brightbridge Ventures
Location: London
Currency: GBP
Size: 50m
Targeting: Europe
Bio: Established to build great fintech companies.
Investment: 1-10m
Website: www.brightbridgeventures.com
Contact email: info@brightbridgeventures.com

Business Growth Fund
Location: London, Aberdeen, Bristol, Birmingham, Edinburgh, Leeds, Manchester
Currency: GBP
Size: 2.5bn
Targeting: UK
Bio: Broad portfolio ranging from healthcare to construction and business services. Invest primarily in growth and the potential for growth across the entire UK.
Investment: 20k - 10m
Portfolio: Broadband Choices, Bullitt, Furniture Village +
Stage: Late Stage
Website: www.businessgrowthfund.co.uk
Contact tel: +44 3452668860

Cambridge Angels
Location: Cambridge
Currency: GBP
Size: 2.5m
Targeting: UK
Bio: Internet, software, technology and bio-technology.
Investment: 50k - 1m
Website: www.cambridgeangels.com
Contact email: info@cambridgeangels.net

Cambridge Associates

Location: London
Targeting: Worldwide
Bio: Leading investment advisor to foundations and endowments, private wealth, and corporate and government entities.
Website: www.cambridgeassociates.com

Company Partners

Bio: Matching service.
Stage: Start-ups
Website: www.companypartners.com
Contact tel: +44 1635202894

Conduit Ventures

Location: London
Targeting: OECD and select Asian companies
Bio: They specialize in high-efficiency energy generation and storage, particularly focusing on low-carbon tech, fuel cells, hydrogen and more.
Investment: 3m
Portfolio: Heliocentris, Protonex, Wal fuel +
Stage: Early & Mid Stage
Website: www.conduit-ventures.com
Contact email: office@conduit-ventures.com
Contact tel: +44 2078313131

Connect Ventures

Location: London
Currency: USD
Size: 33m
Targeting: Europe
Bio: Helping founders build product-centric start-ups (mobile, internet, digital media).
Investment: 300 - 600k
Portfolio: Boiler Room, Soldo, Unmade +
Stage: Early & Mid Stage
Website: www.connectventures.co.uk

Connection Capital

Location: London
Currency: GBP
Size: 170m
Targeting: UK
Bio: Invest in UK companies with strong management teams that are already in profit. They've backed all sorts of companies from gyms to online businesses.
Investment: 2 – 7m
Portfolio: PureGym, Wagamama +
Stage: Late Stage
Website: www.connectioncapital.co.uk
Contact tel: +44 2036964010

Core Growth Capital

Location: London
Website: www.core-cap.com
Contact tel: +44 2031790925

Crescent Capital

Location: Belfast
Currency: USD
Size: 614m
Targeting: Northern Ireland
Bio: Operate in IT, manufacturing and life science sectors. 5-7years.
Investment: 450k - 1.2m
Portfolio: Analytics Engines, Nisoft, SpeechStorm +
Stage: Early & Mid Stage
Website: www.crescentcap.com
Contact tel: +44 2036965420

Crowd Cube

Location: Exeter
Targeting: UK
Website: www.crowdcube.com
Contact email: support@crowdcube.com
Contact tel: +44 1392241319

Dawn Capital

Location: London
Currency: USD
Size: 180m
Targeting: Europe
Bio: Invest in start-ups across Europe, fintech, SaaS, B2B, marketplaces, cloud, cyber security.
Investment: 250k – 10m
Portfolio: iZettle, Bathrooms.com +
Stage: Early Stage
Website: www.dawncapital.com

DN Capital

Location: London, Palo Alto
Currency: USD
Size: 200m
Targeting: UK, North America
Bio: Invests in digital media, e-commerce, software and mobile applications.
Investment: 1 - 10m
Portfolio: Shazam, Lovespace, Happn +
Stage: Late Stage
Website: www.dncapital.com
Contact email: info@dncapital.com
Contact tel: +44 2073401600

Doughty Hanson Technology Fund

Location: London, Frankfurt, Milan, Stockholm, Paris, Luxembourg, Madrid
Currency: EUR
Size: 8bn
Targeting: Europe
Bio: Invest in technology, manufacturing and internet based commerce. Long-term investments throughout the life of the company.
Portfolio: Everbridge, MBA Polymers, Soundbutt +
Stage: Late Stage
Website: www.doughtyhanson.com
Contact email: info@doughtyhanson.com
Contact tel: +44 2076639300

Draper Espirit

Location: London, Cambridge, Dublin
Targeting: UK, Nordics, Germany, France, Ireland, Spain
Bio: Their main focus is across electronics, software, internet, medtech, mobile over a massive geographical area.
Investment: 500k – 15m
Portfolio: Graze, Lyst, Zopa +
Stage: Early & Growth Stage
Website: www.draperesprit.com
Contact tel: +44 2079318800

EC1 Capital

Location: London
Currency: USD
Size: 15m
Targeting: UK
Bio: Invests in mobile and web technology companies.
Investment: 1m
Portfolio: Lifecake, Toothpick, Evvnt +
Stage: Early & Mid Stage
Website: www.ec1capital.com
Contact email: info@ec1capital.com

Eco Machines Ventures

Location: London
Targeting: UK, Europe, CIS, Israel
Bio: Investments in innovative pan-European B2B hardware companies. They foster the development of world-class technology in the energy, transport, circular economy, smart city and industrial high-tech sectors.
Investment: 2m
Portfolio: Recycling Technologies, Q-Bot, NIS, Rotary EcoMachines, PDE, Autorose.
Stage: Early & Mid Stage
Website: www.ecomachinesventures.com
Contact email: info@ecomachinesventures.com
Contact tel: +44 2037616138

Eden Ventures

Location: London
Currency: USD

Size: 98m
Targeting: UK
Bio: Invest in early stage technology companies.
Investment: 200k - 6m
Portfolio: Huddle, UberVU, Reevoo +
Stage: Late Stage
Website: www.edenventures.co.uk
Contact email: info@edenventures.co.uk
Contact tel: +44 2077583440

Edinburgh Partners
Location: Edinburgh
Currency: GBP
Size: 38m
Website: www.edinburghpartners.com
Contact tel: +44 2072972420

Entrepreneurs Fund
Location: London, Jersey
Currency: EUR
Size: 240m
Targeting: Europe
Bio: Invest in all forms of technology and life sciences businesses at all stages of a company's life.
Portfolio: Fits.Me, Realeyes, N-TEC +
Stage: Seed, Early Stage, Later Stage and Post IPO Equity Investments
Website: www.entrepreneursfund.com
Contact email: info@entrepreneursfund.com
Contact tel: +44 2073551011

Episode1
Location: London
Currency: USD
Size: 60m
Targeting: UK
Bio: Set up to support fund managers who invest in small, high-growth, software-driven businesses.
Investment: 250k - 2m

Portfolio: Touch Surgery, Global App Testing, Carwow +
Stage: Early & Mid Stage
Website: www.episode1.com
Contact email: info@episode1.com

Force Overmass Capital
Location: London
Bio: Software and hardware.
Website: www.fomcap.com
Contact email: info@fomcap.com
Contact tel: +44 2034179839

Forward Partners
Location: London
Currency: USD
Size: 9m
Targeting: UK
Bio: Forward Partners specialise in helping e-commerce platforms dominate their niche.
Portfolio: Appear Here, Lexoo, Lost My Name +
Stage: Early & Mid Stage
Website: www.forwardpartners.com

Frog Capital
Location: London
Currency: EUR
Size: 1bn
Targeting: Europe
Bio: Invest in IT, digital media & resource efficiency.
Investment: 5 - 25m
Portfolio: Editd, Rated People, Ostara +
Stage: Late Stage
Website: www.frogcapital.com
Contact tel: +44 2078330555

Frontline Ventures
Location: London
Currency: USD
Size: 54m

Targeting: Europe
Bio: Focus on Seed and Series A Internet/software companies.
Investment: 100k – 2.5m
Portfolio: CurrencyFair, Boxever, Orchestrate, Drop, Logentries, Qstream, Boxfish
Stage: Early & Mid Stage
Website: www.frontline.vc

Horatio Investments

Location: Glastonbury
Currency: GBP
Size: 100m
Targeting: UK
Bio: Family office investing in financial services and renewable energy Technologies.
Investment: 500k
Portfolio: Csabu, ThinkBuzan, Witlr +
Stage: Early Stage
Website: www.horatioinvestments.com
Contact tel: +44 2033978870

Howzat Partners

Location: London
Currency: USD
Size: 10m
Targeting: UK
Bio: Specialising in: retail, Media, photography and technology.
Investment: 10m
Portfolio: Alex and Alexa, Swapit, Fantasy 5 Live +
Stage: Late Stage
Website: www.howzatpartners.com
Contact email: info@howzatpartners.com

Hoxton Ventures

Location: London
Currency: USD
Size: 47m
Targeting: Europe
Bio: Invest in technology (internet and software). Mid length 7-10 years.

Investment: 250k – 2m
Portfolio: Raptor Supplies, Deliveroo, Campanja +
Stage: Early & Mid Stage
Website: www.hoxtonventures.com
Contact email: businessplans@hoxton.vc

Imperial Innovations
Location: London
Currency: GBP
Size: 60m
Targeting: UK
Bio: Technology commercialisation and venture capital investor focused on technology arising from the UK's four leading universities.
Investment: 10k - 25m
Stage: Seed, Early, Late
Website: www.imperialinnovations.co.uk
Contact tel: +44 2030538850

Index Ventures
Location: London, San Francisco, Geneva
Currency: USD
Size: 706m
Targeting: Worldwide
Bio: Supports the founders of companies who are looking to be the Fortune 500 of the next 50 years. Invests in both technology and healthcare.
Investment: 250k - 50m
Portfolio: Dropbox, Facebook, Skype +
Stage: Late Stage
Website: www.indexventures.com
Contact tel: +44 2071542020

Initial Capital
Location: London, Silicon Valley
Targeting: UK, Europe & USA
Bio: Specialises in consumer services, mobile software and games.
Portfolio: Super Evil Megacorp, Supercell, appGyver +

Stage: Early & Mid Stage
Website: www.initialcapital.com
Contact email: info@initialcapital.com

Iona Capital
Location: London
Currency: USD
Size: 8m
Targeting: UK, Europe
Bio: Technology, internet, cloud computing, software, mobile computing.
Investment: 500k - 10m
Website: www.ionacapital.co.uk
Contact email: info@ionacapital.co.uk
Contact tel: +44 2070643300

JamJar Investments
Location: London
Targeting: UK
Bio: Aim to help bring your company up from an initial base to a major organisation, with your customers at the forefront.
Investment: 150k – 1m
Portfolio: Graze, Toucan Box, Pop Chips +
Stage: Early & Mid Stage
Website: www.jamjarinvestments.com
Contact email: bread@jamjarinvestments.com

Joy Capital
Location: Middlesex
Website: www.joycapital.com
Contact email: contact@joycapital.com

Kennet Partners
Location: London
Currency: USD
Size: 314m
Targeting: Europe, United Kingdom, United States
Bio: Software, enterprise software, advertising.

Investment: 10 - 50m
Portfolio: Rivo, World One, Spreadshirt
Stage: Early and Late Stage
Website: www.kennet.com
Contact tel: +44 2030043250

Kreos Capital
Location: London
Currency: USD
Size: 752m
Targeting: Austria, Belgium, Denmark, Finland, France, Germany, Ireland, Israel, Italy, Netherlands, Spain, Sweden, UK, USA
Bio: Debt provider – in fact they're Europe's largest and leading debt provider. Kreos have commited in excess of EUR 1 billion to the automotive, finance and services industries.
Investment: 1 - 10m
Portfolio: Borro, Codemasters, Wonga +
Stage: Late Stage
Website: www.kreoscapital.com
Contact email: info@kreoscapital.com
Contact tel: +44 2077583450

Lean Investments
Location: London
Targeting: UK, Europe
Bio: Invests in technology and internet while differentiating with a personalised approach.
Investment: 500k - 1m
Stage: Early & Mid Stage
Website: www.leaninvestments.com

London Venture Partners
Location: London
Currency: USD
Size: 40bn
Targeting: UK
Bio: Invests in online, social, mobile and tablet games.
Investment: 20k - 2m
Portfolio: Omnidrone, Applifier, PlayRaven +

Stage: Early & Mid Stage
Website: www.londonvp.com
Contact email: pitch@londonvp.com

Longwall Ventures
Location: Oxford
Currency: USD
Size: 63m
Targeting: UK
Bio: Focuses on healthcare, engineering and science start-ups.
Portfolio: Crysalin, Ibexis,microVISC +
Stage: Early & Mid Stage
Website: www.longwallventures.com
Contact email: contact@longwallventures.com
Contact tel: +44 1235567365

Martlet Corporate Angel
Location: Cambridge
Targeting: UK
Bio: Typically involved with software, electronics, medtech and similar.
Investment: 10 - 100k
Portfolio: Converge, Repositive, Artfinder +
Stage: Early & Mid Stage
Website: www.martlet-angel.com

Maven Capital Partners
Location: London, Aberdeen, Birmingham, Edinburgh, Glasgow, Manchester
Currency: GBP
Size: 380m
Targeting: UK
Bio: has invested in clean technology, hardware, software and messaging services for a decade.
Portfolio: RMEC Ltd, Vermilion, DMACK Tyres +
Stage: Late Stage
Website: www.mavencp.com
Contact tel: +44 2031022750

Mercia Fund Management

Location: Henley
Currency: USD
Size: 5m
Targeting: UK
Bio: Provides growth capital for early-stage ventures that have demonstrated some commercial traction, as well as post-investment support, including an incubator accommodation at Forward House.
Investment: 50 - 250m
Portfolio: Crowd Reactive, Kwanji, Sarissa Biomedical +
Stage: Early & Mid Stage
Website: www.merciafund.co.uk
Contact email: info@merciafund.co.uk
Contact tel: +44 3302231430

MMC Ventures

Location: London
Currency: USD
Size: 155m
Targeting: UK
Bio: Media internet, financial services and software. Do not invest in start-ups and also avoid capital intensive businesses.
Investment: 500k - 4m
Portfolio: Bottica, LoveHomeSwap +
Stage: Early & Mid Stage
Website: www.mmcventures.com
Contact tel: +44 2079382220

Mosaic Ventures

Location: London
Currency: USD
Size: 140m
Targeting: Europe, USA
Bio: They focus on several key areas, including market places, SaaS for SMEs, next-gen finance and payments, analytics, education, health and bitcoins.
Portfolio: Blockchain, Number Four, Guevara +
Stage: Late Stage
Website: www.mosaicventures.com
Contact email: info@mosaicventures.com

MVM Life Science Partners
Location: London, Boston
Currency: USD
Size: 225m
Targeting: Europe, USA
Bio: Investing in emerging healthcare companies since 1998.
Investment: 5 - 20m
Portfolio: Exits include BioVex, Aegerion, Momenta, PregLem, Domanti +
Stage: Late Stage
Website: www.mvm.com
Contact email: hh@mvm.com
Contact tel: +44 2079382220

North West Fund, The
Location: Warrington
Currency: GBP
Size: 155m
Targeting: UK
Bio: Biotechnology, healthcare, clean technology.
Investment: 50k - 2m
Portfolio: Compliance Control, Bioxyden, moplex +
Website: www.thenorthwestfund.co.uk
Contact tel: +44 1925418232

Notion Capital
Location: London, New York
Currency: USD
Size: 270m
Targeting: Europe
Bio: Focussing on B2B Butt and SaaS companies from Seed to Series A.
Portfolio: Shutl, Duedil, Shopa
Stage: Late Stage
Website: www.notion.vc
Contact email: info@notioncapital.com
Contact tel: +44 8454989393

NVM Private Equity Limited
Location: Newcastle
Currency: USD
Size: 31m
Targeting: UK
Bio: Invests in all sectors: healthcare and biotechnology, computer and electronics, information technology services, construction, consumer, industrial and manufacturing.
Investment: 2 - 10m
Stage: Growth and Late Ventures
Website: www.nvm.co.uk
Contact email: wendy.arkle@nvm.co.uk
Contact tel: +44 1912446024

Octopus Ventures
Location: London
Currency: USD
Size: 669m
Targeting: UK
Bio: Specialise in renewable energy, healthcare and property finance.
Investment: 250k - 100m
Portfolio: YPlan, Secret Escapes, Zoopla +
Stage: Late Stage
Website: www.octopusinvestments.com
Contact tel: +44 8003162295

Orange Growth Capital
Location: London, Amsterdam
Targeting: Europe, Middle East, Africa
Bio: Fintech focused investment firm.
Investment: 250k - 10m
Portfolio: Salviol, Zopa and Knip +
Website: www.ogc-partners.com
Contact email: info@ogc-partners.com

Oxford Capital Partners
Location: Oxford
Currency: USD

Size: 390m
Targeting: UK
Bio: Invests in biotechnology, software, hardware.
Investment: 500k - 10m
Stage: Early - Late
Website: www.oxcp.com
Contact email: info@oxcp.com
Contact tel: +44 1865860760

Panoramic Growth Equity
Location: London
Currency: USD
Size: 51m
Targeting: UK
Bio: Invest in UK growth SMEs across all mainstream sectors. Software, consulting, advertising, business services, media, travel.
Investment: 500k - 2.5m
Stage: Late Stage
Website: www.pgequity.com
Contact email: team@pgequity.com
Contact tel: +44 2071003715

Par Equity
Location: Edinburgh
Targeting: UK
Bio: They aim to bring a wealth of knowledge under the 'Par Umbrella', helping you unlock your entrepreneurial potential.
Portfolio: Covec, miiCard, KILTR +
Stage: Early & Mid Stage
Website: www.parequity.com
Contact email: mandy.porteous@parequity.com
Contact tel: +44 1315560044

Passion Capital
Location: London
Currency: USD
Size: 390m
Targeting: UK

Investment: 50k +
Portfolio: EyeEm, Mendeley, Loopcam +
Stage: Early & Mid Stage
Website: www.passioncapital.com
Contact tel: +44 2078333373

Pentech Ventures

Location: London, Edinburgh
Currency: USD
Size: 122m
Targeting: UK, Ireland
Bio: Invest in technology companies that are disrupting social media, e-commerce, digital media, mobile, SaaS and more.
Investment: 500k - 4m
Stage: Early & Mid Stage
Website: www.pentech.vc
Contact email: info@pentechvc.com
Contact tel: +44 2031287473

Piton Capital

Location: London
Currency: USD
Size: 28m
Targeting: Europe
Bio: Invest in online marketplaces, network economics, exchange and social networks.
Investment: 200k - 15m
Portfolio: Autotrader, Betfair and QXL Ricardo +
Stage: Early & Mid Stage
Website: www.pitoncap.com
Contact email: info@pitoncap.com
Contact tel: +44 2074080451

Playfair Capital

Location: London
Currency: USD
Size: 15m
Targeting: UK, Europe, USA, Africa

Bio: Backs technology and consumer based start-ups as an early stage investor.
Investment: 30 - 300k
Portfolio: DueDil, Mixlr, F6S +
Stage: Early & Mid Stage
Website: www.playfaircapital.com

Pond Ventures

Location: London, Silicon Valley, Israel
Currency: USD
Size: 200m
Targeting: North America, UK, Israel
Bio: Europe's largest early stage technology VC fund.
Portfolio: Swapit, Acco, LiveRail +
Stage: Early & Mid Stage
Website: www.pondventures.com
Contact tel: +44 2089401001

PROfounders Capital

Location: London
Targeting: Europe
Bio: VC fund powered by entrepreneurs. Their investors and principles have built some of Europe's most successful companies including lastminute.com, Bebo and TopTable.
Investment: 500k - 2.5m
Portfolio: made.com, TweetDeck, easyCar +
Stage: Early & Mid Stage
Website: www.profounderscapital.com
Contact tel: +44 2077666900

Reed Elsevier Ventures

Location: London
Currency: USD
Size: 200m
Targeting: Europe, UK, USA, Israel
Bio: Sectors: Analytics, apps, advertising.
Investment: 1 - 10m
Stage: Series A or B
Website: www.reedelsevierventures.com

Contact email: luke.smith@reedelsevier.com
Contact tel: +44 2071665665

Regional Growth Fund
Location: UK
Currency: USD
Size: 484m
Targeting: UK
Bio: Regional Growth Fund is a British Government initiative to help fund UK businesses.
Investment: 1m
Website: www.gov.uk
Contact email: growthfund@bis.gsi.gov.uk

SaatchInvest
Location: London
Targeting: UK
Bio: SaatchInvest help products get to market quicker by investing in micro VC.
Investment: 100 - 300k
Portfolio: Evrythng, TouchCast, Hatch +
Stage: Early & Mid Stage
Website: www.saatchinvest.com
Contact email: newdeals@saatchinvest.co.uk

Santander InnoVentures
Location: London
Currency: USD
Size: 100m
Bio: Aims to help fintech companies grow from a very early stage to a more mature stage.
Portfolio: iZettle, MyCheck, Cyanogen, Ripple and Kabbage +
Website: www.santanderinnoventures.com
Contact email: info@santanderinnoventures.com

Seed Camp
Location: London
Currency: USD
Size: 39m

Bio: Invest in technology-oriented companies and are largely industry agnostic.
Investment: 300k - 2m
Stage: Seed
Website: www.seedcamp.com
Contact email: info@seedcamp.com

SEIS Seed Enterprise Investment Scheme
Location: London
Website: www.seis.co.uk

SEP (Scottish Equity Partners)
Location: London, Glasgow, Edinburgh
Currency: GBP
Size: 35m
Targeting: UK
Bio: Looking to invest in UK based companies addressing international markets in the technology space.
Investment: 1 - 20m
Portfolio: Skyscanner, Car Loan 4U, matches fashion +
Stage: Late Stage
Website: www.sep.co.uk
Contact email: enquiries@sep.co.uk
Contact tel: +44 2077585900

SPARK Ventures
Location: London
Targeting: UK
Bio: Invests in TMT (technology, media and telecom) and healthcare businesses.
Investment: 500k - 2m
Portfolio: Firebox, Mind Candy +
Stage: Early & Mid Stage
Website: www.sparkventures.com
Contact email: enquiries@sparkventures.com

Startupbootcamp - accelerator
Location: London (17 locations overall)
Targeting: Worldwide
Bio: 20+ accelerator programs Four Scale programs for growth-stage companies

Corporate Innovation. The industry focus areas are fintech and financial inclusion insurtech, Smart City, digital health, foodrech, IoT, energy & sustainability, cybersecurity, sportstech, artificial intelligence and commerce.

Investment: 550k +

Website: www.startupbootcamp.org

Contact email: info@startupbootcamp.org

Summit Partners

Location: London

Currency: USD

Size: 16bn

Targeting: UK, USA

Bio: Invest in technology, life sciences and growth products.

Investment: 5m - 5bn

Portfolio: Acturis, ApoCell, Belkin +

Stage: Late Stage

Website: www.summitpartners.com

Contact tel: +44 2076597500

Supremum Capital

Location: London

Targeting: Europe, Russia

Bio: Investments in Fintech, internet and real estate sectors, and provides advisory services to their portfolio companies.

Portfolio: Atosho, InPlat, Webbankir +

Stage: Early & Mid Stage

Website: www.supremum-capital.com

Contact email: info@supremum-capital.com

Sussex Place Ventures

Location: London

Currency: USD

Size: 51m

Targeting: UK

Bio: Focus on information technology and businesses with patent-protected tech.

Investment: 1m

Portfolio: Sine Wave Entertainment, Infinitesima, Skimlinks +

Stage: Early & Mid Stage

Website: www.spventures.com
Contact email: info@spventures.com
Contact tel: +44 2070000022

Thames Valley Capital
Location: London
Bio: Targets companies with a focus on media, first mover advantage including FMCG, lifestyle and green technology.
Investment: 50k - 5m
Stage: Seed, Early & Late
Website: www.tvcapital.co.uk
Contact email: info@tvcapital.co.uk
Contact tel: +44 1189001523

Venatus Interactive PLC
Location: London
Bio: Invest in up and coming companies in the interactive gaming industry, as well as investing in current established gaming businesses with a proven track record of strong returns.
Stage: Early & Mid Stage
Contact tel: +44 2070999646

Wellington Partners
Location: London, Munich, Zurich, Palo Alto
Currency: USD
Size: 592m
Targeting: Worldwide
Bio: Wellington focus on digital media and butt-based software.
Investment: 500k - 20m
Portfolio: Hailo, Dropbox, Import.io +
Stage: Early & Mid Stage
Website: www.wellington-partners.com

White Star Capital
Location: London
Currency: USD
Size: 70m
Targeting: Europe, USA

Bio: Investment company for digital and mobile technology start-ups.
Investment: 500k - 5m
Portfolio: KeyMe, DICE, Dollar Shave Club +
Stage: Early & Mid Stage
Website: www.whitestarvc.com
Contact email: info@whitestarvc.com

YFM Equity Partners
Location: Leeds
Targeting: UK
Bio: Invests in SMEs and companies across a range of sectors and has a particular interest in energy, healthcare and technology.
Investment: 100k - 5m
Stage: Late Stage
Website: www.yfmep.com
Contact email: info@yfmep.com
Contact tel: +44 2034409045

2.3

UK ANGEL NETWORKS

Accelerator Academy
Location: London
Bio: Tech/Media/Telecoms (specifically includes SaaS, commerce, mobile apps, web platforms, marketplaces, edtech, adtech, fintech, big data, cloud, analytics etc.). Excludes medtech, bioscience / lifescience.
Investment: 150k
Business Type/Stage: Early Stage
Website: www.acceleratoracademy.com
Contact tel: +44 2032803705

Advantage Business Angels
Location: Birmingham
Coverage: National
Bio: Built a reputation for integrity and success in securing equity finance for companies at all stages, and in all sectors, to grow and succeed; including rescue and recovery situations.
Investment: 150k - 1m
Business Type/Stage: Early Stage
Website: www.advantagebusinessangels.com
Contact email: bob.barnsley@abangels.com

Advantage Business Partnerships
Business Type/Stage: Early Stage
Website: www.advantagebusinessltd.com
Contact tel: +44 2033840276

Angel Investment Network
Location: London
Currency: GBP
Size: 50k - 1m
Coverage: Global network of angel investors with 35 websites covering over 70 countries.
Website: www.angelinvestmentnetwork.co.uk

AngelList
Location: London
Coverage: National
Bio: Sectors considered: early stage technology
Investment: 150k - 3m
Business Type/Stage: Early Stage
Website: www.angel.co
Contact email: team@angel.co

AngelNews
Business Type/Stage: Early Stage
Website: www.angelnewsletter.co.uk
Contact email: fuchsia@angelnews.co.uk
Contact tel: +44 1749344888

Angels Academe
Coverage: National
Bio: Sectors considered: digital media, fintech, retail tech
Investment: 150 - 500k
Business Type/Stage: UK businesses with £1-3m pre-money valuation. Early Stage.
Website: www.angelacademe.com

Angel CoFund
Location: Sheffield
Coverage: UK
Bio: Angel CoFund invests in small and medium-sized enterprises with high growth potential across the UK. E-commerce, biotechnology, clean technology.
Investment: 100m
Business Type/Stage: Adventoris, Hopster +
Website: www.angelcofund.co.uk
Contact email: info@angelcofund.co.uk

Angels Den
Location: St. Albans
Coverage: Worldwide
Bio: Invest in pre-vetted SMEs.
Investment: 50k
Business Type/Stage: Early Stage
Website: www.angelsden.com
Contact email: info@angelsden.com
Contact tel: +44 2033180230

Angels Unleashed
Location: Kent
Coverage: National, international
Bio: Invest in early stage start-ups.
Business Type/Stage: Early Stage
Website: www.angelsunleashed.co.uk

Anglia Capital Group
Coverage: South East
Bio: Investing in hi-tech businesses and technology start-ups since 2001.
Business Type/Stage: Early Stage
Website: www.angliacapitalgroup.co.uk

Anvil Partners LLP
Location: London
Coverage: National
Bio: Sectors considered: EIS, biomedical, education
Investment: 150 - 500k

Business Type/Stage: Early Stage
Website: www.anvilpartners.co.uk
Contact email: michaelanvilpartners@mac.com

Asset Match Limited

Location: London
Coverage: National
Bio: Focused on providing growing and profitable companies with reliable liquidity in their securities.
Business Type/Stage: Early Stage
Website: www.assetmatch.com
Contact email: info@assetmatch.com
Contact tel: +44 2072482788

Avonmore Developments Ltd

Location: London
Coverage: National
Bio: Sectors considered: Advertising, digital media, ICT, mobile tech, software, internet, retail, media
Investment: 50 - 250k
Business Type/Stage: Businesses with sub- £3m pre-money valuations. Early stage.
Website: www.avonmoredevelopments.com
Contact email: contactus@avonmoredevelopments.com
Contact tel: +44 2070027718

Azini Capital

Location: London
Coverage: National
Bio: Sectors considered: Technology & technology-enabled businesses
Investment: 3m
Business Type/Stage: Minimum of USD 10m of revenue. Late stage.
Website: www.azini.com
Contact email: info@azini.com
Contact tel: +44 2073193900

BnkToThe Future

Location: London
Coverage: National

Bio: Support you in getting crowd-investment ready including business plan, financial model, valuation, pitch video, legals etc.
Investment: 150k - 3m
Website: www.bnktothefuture.com
Contact email: info@banktothefuture.com

BBA - British Bankers Association
Location: London
Coverage: National
Website: www.bba.org.uk
Contact tel: +44 2072168800

Beaufort Securities Limited
Location: London
Coverage: England
Website: www.beaufortsecurities.com
Contact tel: +44 2073828300

Beauhurst
Location: London
Coverage: National
Website: www.about.beauhurst.com
Contact tel: +44 8006126768

Beavis Morgan
Location: London
Coverage: National
Website: www.beavismorgan.com
Contact email: london@beavismorgan.com
Contact tel: +44 2074170417

Beer & Young
Location: London
Coverage: National
Investment: 250k - 3m
Business Type/Stage: SMEs, Start-ups and Late Stage.
Website: www.beerandyoung.com
Contact email: info@beerandyoung.com
Contact tel: +44 2076377755

Bovill

Location: London
Coverage: National
Website: www.bovill.com
Contact email: enquiries@bovill.com
Contact tel: +44 2076377755

Business Agent

Coverage: National
Bio: Combines various types of funding including Equity Crowdfunding, Debt Based Crowdfunding and Property Crowdfunding.
Website: www.businessagent.com

Business Growth Fund

Location: London
Currency: USD
Size: 310m
Coverage: National
Bio: Invests in SMEs focussing on e-commerce, software, manufacturing.
Investment: 2 - 10m
Business Type/Stage: Early Stage
Website: www.businessgrowthfund.co.uk
Contact tel: +44 3452668860

Cambridge Capital Group

Location: Cambridge
Coverage: International
Bio: Sectors considered: High tech
Investment: 150 - 250k
Business Type/Stage: Start-up
Website: www.cambridgecapitalgroup.co.uk

Cass Entrepreneuship Fund

Coverage: London, South East
Bio: Sectors considered: ICT, medtech, biotechnology, clean technology, energy, services and business services
Investment: 150 - 500k
Business Type/Stage: Start-up

Website: www.cass.city.ac.uk
Contact email: helen.reynolds@city.ac.uk
Contact tel: +44 2070408972

Catapult Venture Managers Ltd
Location: Leicester
Coverage: National
Bio: Sectors considered: healthcare and pharmaceuticals, luxury consumer brands, manufacturing and software.
Investment: 200k - 2m
Website: www.catapult-ventures.com
Contact tel: +44 1162388200

Charlotte Street Capital
Coverage: National
Bio: Sectors considered: Technology
Investment: 150 - 250k
Business Type/Stage: Early Stage
Website: www.charlottestreetcapital.com
Contact email: tom@charlottestreetcapital.com

Clearly Social Angels
Coverage: National
Bio: Look for unusually talented teams intent on building businesses that can scale explosively to create, transform or dominate an industry.
Investment: 150 - 250k
Website: www.clearlyso.com

Colnvestor
Location: London
Coverage: National
Bio: Sectors considered: All EIS Qualifying sectors
Investment: 150k - 1m

Compare Investments Dot Guru
Bio: Investors interested in the SEIS, EIS, VCT and BPR alternative investment marketplace, and bring together all publicly available investment opportunities into one searchable and comparable database.

Website: www.compareinvestments.guru
Contact email: guru@compareinvestments.guru
Contact tel: +44 2079935307

Connect London

Location: London
Coverage: London
Investment: 150k - 3m
Website: www.connectlondon.org
Contact email: info@connectlondon.org
Contact tel: +44 2070363991

Crowd2Fund

Coverage: National
Bio: Allows investors and businesses to raise and invest using five different crowdfunding models which include: loans, equity, revenue, rewards and donations.
Investment: 500k - 3m
Website: www.crowd2fund.com
Contact email: info@crowd2fund.com
Contact tel: +44 2035070073

CrowdBnk

Location: London
Coverage: National
Investment: 500k - 3m
Website: www.crowdbnk.com
Contact email: contactus@crowdbnk.com
Contact tel: +44 2032891494

Crowdcube

Location: Exeter
Coverage: National
Bio: Platform where entrepreneurs can showcase their business's investment potential to a nation of 'Armchair Dragon' investors in return for equity.
Investment: 150 - 500k
Website: www.crowdcube.com
Contact email: support@crowdcube.com
Contact tel: +44 1392241319

DC Consulting

Location: Scotland
Coverage: National
Investment: 250k - 25m
Website: www.dcconsult.co.uk
Contact tel: +44 1382339290

Deloitte LLP

Location: London
Coverage: National
Website: www2.deloitte.com

Dorset Business Angels

Location: Dorset
Coverage: South West, Thames Valley, Wales
Investment: 150k - 1m
Business Type/Stage: Seed
Website: dorsetbusinessangels.co.uk
Contact email: contact@dorsetbusinessangels.co.uk
Contact tel: +44 120270697

E2Exchange

Location: London
Coverage: National
Investment: 150k - 3m
Website: e2exchange.com
Contact email: info@e2exchange.com
Contact tel: +44 2030785866

EC1 Capital Limited

Location: London
Currency: GBP
Size: 10m
Coverage: National
Investment: 150 - 250k
Website: www.ec1capital.com
Contact email: info@ec1capital.com

ECI Partners LLP
Location: London
Coverage: National
Business Type/Stage: Companies valued between GBP 10 - 150 m
Website: www.ecipartners.com
Contact tel: +44 2076061000

EcoMachines Ventures Limited
Location: London
Coverage: National, European, International
Bio: Sectors considered: Cleantech including energy, transportation, smart city, circular economy and industrial high-tech.
Investment: 150k - 3m
Website: www.ecomachinesventures.com
Contact email: info@ecomachinesventures.com
Contact tel: +44 2037616138

e-Man
Location: London
Website: www.e-man.co.uk
Contact email: info@e-man.co.uk

Emerging Payments Association
Coverage: National
Bio: Special focus on fintech.
Website: www.emergingpayments.org
Contact tel: +44 2073789890

Entrepreneurial Finance Hub
Location: Lancashire
Coverage: International
Website: www.biginnovationcentre.com
Contact email: info@entrepreneurialfinancehub.com

Entrepreneurial-Spark
Coverage: National
Business Type/Stage: Businesses with GBP 1m turnover.
Website: www.entrepreneurial-spark.com

Contact email: hello@entrepreneurial-spark.com
Contact tel: +44 1414189120

Envestors
Location: Envestors
Coverage: National, European, International
Bio: Preference towards: b2b, technology, media, communications, clean-tech, energy, mobile, medtech, manufacturing outsourcing and product/service innovation.
Investment: 150k - 3m
Website: www.envestors.envestry.com
Contact email: info@envestors.co.uk
Contact tel: +44 2072400202

Episode 1 Ventures
Location: London
Coverage: National, European
Bio: Sectors considered: ICT, Medtech
Investment: 250k - 1m
Business Type/Stage: Early Stage
Website: www.episode1.com
Contact email: info@episode1.com

Finance Wales
Location: Cardiff
Coverage: Wales
Bio: Software, manufacturing, health care
Investment: 1k- 2m
Business Type/Stage: Start-ups & Early Stage
Website: www.financewales.co.uk
Contact tel: +44 8005874140

Finanziaconnect
Location: UK, Spain
Coverage: National, European
Website: www.finanziaconnect.com
Contact email: finanziapyme@finanziapyme.es

FINTECH Circle
Coverage: National
Bio: Sectors Considered: Fintech and software
Investment: 150 - 500k
Website: www.fintechcircle.com
Contact email: info@fintechcircle.com

Forward Partners
Location: London
Coverage: National
Bio: Sectors Considered: Seed and Start-up e-commerce, marketplace and related software.
Investment: 250 - 500k
Website: www.forwardpartners.com
Contact email: social@forwardpartners.com

Funding Tree
Coverage: National
Bio: Offer both equity and debt investment opportunities via a simple-to use online platform.
Investment: 150k - 3m
Website: www.fundingtree.co.uk
Contact email: contact@fundingtree.co.uk
Contact tel: +44 2071831426

Gabriel Investors
Coverage: North East
Bio: Very interested in EIS deals.
Investment: 150k
Website: www.gabriel-investors.com
Contact email: archangel@gabriel-investors.com

Green Angel Syndicate
Location: Edinburgh
Coverage: National, International
Bio: Sectors considered: Companies of benefit to the Green Economy, with specific reference to the water and energy sectors.
Investment: 150 - 500k

Website: www.greenangelsyndicate.com
Contact email: nicklyth@gasgat.com

Growth Accelerator
Coverage: England
Bio: Growth Accelerator exclusively targets high growth businesses who want to enter their next growth phase and have the potential and determination to get there.
Business Type/Stage: Service based SMEs.
Website: www.greatbusiness.gov.uk
Contact email: enquiries@growthaccelerator.com

Growthdeck Ltd
Coverage: National
Bio: Equity investment platform that helps you invest in quality UK companies in the right way.
Investment: 500k - 1m
Website: www.growthdeck.com
Contact email: info@growthdeck.com

Halo
Location: Belfast
Currency: GBP
Size: 4.5m
Coverage: Northern Ireland
Bio: Sectors considered: All except straight retail (shops) and property.
Investment: 150 - 500k
Website: www.haloim.com
Contact tel: +44 2890737814

Harbottle & Lewis
Location: London
Coverage: National
Bio: Specializes in media and entertainment and provides a complete range of commercial advice to entrepreneurs and companies.
Business Type/Stage: Start-ups & large corporates
Website: www.harbottle.com
Contact tel: +44 2076675000

Harvard Business Angels

Coverage: UK, US, Europe
Bio: Support the rapidly growing UK start-up ecosystem.
Business Type/Stage: Early and growing
Website: www.hbsa.org.uk
Contact email: admin@hbsa-angelslondon.org.uk

HoxTech Angels

Coverage: International
Bio: Sectors considered: Technology
Investment: 150 - 500k
Business Type/Stage: Start-ups
Website: www.hoxtechangels.com
Contact tel: +44 7810155810

ICEX Spain Trade and Investement

Location: London
Coverage: National
Bio: ICEX Spain Trade and Investment is a Spanish public corporation whose mission is to promote Spanish companies and exports, as well as to attract foreign investment to Spain.
Website: www.investinspain.org
Contact email: buzon.inversiones@comercio.mineco.es
Contact tel: +44 2077767730

Ignite

Location: Newcastle
Currency: GBP
Size: 10m
Coverage: National
Bio: Sectors considered: Technology
Investment: 17k
Business Type/Stage: Early Stage
Website: www.ignite.io
Contact email: hello@ignite.io

Incubate London

Location: London
Coverage: National

Bio: Sectors considered: Fintech, technology start-ups
Business Type/Stage: 10 SMEs per year
Website: www.incubatelondon.com
Contact email: info@incubatelondon.com

Indielab Ltd
Location: London
Coverage: National
Bio: Offering the most exciting and ambitious new TV companies a three-month programme of high-level masterclasses and workshops from industry leaders.
Investment: 2m
Business Type/Stage: TV company start-ups. 15-30 SMEs a year
Website: www.weareindielab.co.uk
Contact email: info@weareindielab.co.uk

Inngot
Location: Swansea
Coverage: National
Bio: Provides web tools to help companies and investors identify and value intellectual property.
Business Type/Stage: Early Stage
Website: www.inngot.com
Contact email: info@inngot.com
Contact tel: +44 3338008090

Innovate UK
Location: Swindon
Coverage: National
Bio: Stimulates technology-enabled innovation in the areas which offer the greatest scope for boosting UK growth and productivity.
Business Type/Stage: Growth Stage
Website: www.gov.uk
Contact email: support@innovateuk.gov.uk

Intelligent Crowd TV
Location: London
Coverage: National

Bio: Focus on scalable businesses with strong management teams and international markets, across any sector, and prefer at least some element of SEIS.
Investment: 150k - 1m
Business Type/Stage: Early Stage
Website: www.intelligentcrowd.tv
Contact tel: +44 7785276703

Invent Network
Coverage: National
Bio: Represents a fresh, new approach for potential high-growth companies to help them grow their business to the next stage.
Investment: 150k - 3m
Business Type/Stage: Growth Stage
Website: www.inventnetwork.co.uk
Contact email: phopkinson@inventnetwork.co.uk
Contact tel: +44 7770756779

InvestingZone
Location: London
Coverage: National
Bio: Provides access to some of the UK's best intuitionally backed equity investments.
Investment: 150k - 1m
Website: www.investingzone.com
Contact email: help@investingzone.com

IQ Capital
Location: Cambridge
Currency: GBP
Size: 25m
Coverage: National
Bio: Invests in high-tech businesses, as well as fast growing companies in more traditional sectors throughout the UK.
Investment: 150k - 3m
Business Type/Stage: Seed and Early Stage
Website: www.iqcapital.co.uk
Contact email: enquiries@iqcapital.co.uk

Ironbridge Capital Partners LLP
Location: London
Coverage: London
Bio: Strategic investor and adviser that works with high-growth businesses to fulfil their potential.
Business Type/Stage: All stages
Website: www.ironbridgecp.com
Contact email: deals@ironbridgecp.com
Contact tel: +44 2033843810

I-Start
Coverage: National, European
Bio: Provides advice on innovation, business models, business planning, market entry strategies, techonology assessment and access to capital markets.
Business Type/Stage: Seed for growth
Website: www.i-start.co.uk
Contact email: info@i-start.co.uk

IW Capital Ltd
Coverage: National
Bio: Provides tax efficient investments to their network of high net worth individuals, family offices, wealth managers and IFAs.
Investment: 150k - 3m
Business Type/Stage: SMEs
Website: www.iwcapital.co.uk
Contact email: info@iwcapital.co.uk
Contact tel: +44 2070152250

JamJar Investments
Location: London
Coverage: National, European
Bio: Sectors considered: Consumer products and services, both consumer tech and consumer offline.
Investment: 150 - 500k
Business Type/Stage: Seed, Series A
Website: www.jamjarinvestments.com
Contact email: bread@jamjarinvestments.com

Jersey Enterprise

Location: Jersey
Coverage: South East
Bio: Grows the economy by assisting Jersey entrepreneurs and businesses to succeed and encouraging new investment into Jersey.
Website: www.jerseybusiness.je
Contact tel: +44 1534448934

Juno Syndicate

Location: London
Coverage: National
Bio: Pools money to make large investments, mentor entrepreneurs and make introductions that can help accelerate growth. EIS qualifying.
Investment: 500k - 3m
Business Type/Stage: Early Stage
Website: www.junocapital.co.uk
Contact tel: +44 2073213752

JustInvesting

Location: London
Coverage: National, European, International
Bio: Online platform which enables investors and entrepreneurs to run an investment process entirely online. And, critically, it also provides ongoing support for the relationship post-funding.
Business Type/Stage: Early Stage
Website: www.justinvesting.com

Kingston Smith

Location: London
Coverage: National (Primarily South East)
Bio: Helping and advising owner-managed businesses of all sizes, as well as not for profit organisations and private clients.
Business Type/Stage: SMEs
Website: www.kingstonsmith.co.uk
Contact tel: +44 2073044646

KPMG

Coverage: National
Bio: KPMG has a skilled team of advisers who have a reputation for delivering forward thinking and objective advice.
Website: www.kpmg.com

LARK

Coverage: National
Bio: Assists both Angel investors and those looking for investment.
Website: www.larkinsurance.co.uk
Contact email: eloise.morgan@larkinsurance.co.uk

Leopard Rock Capital

Location: London
Coverage: National, European
Bio: Provides corporate financial advice and capital raising services for private companies, alternative asset managers and private equity funds.
Investment: 1 - 3m
Website: www.leopardrockcapital.com
Contact email: info@leopardrockcapital.com

Liquidity Limited

Location: London
Coverage: National, European, International
Bio: Provides qualified investors access to high-growth private companies, enabling them to contact and negotiate with existing shareholders that have the support of the company to sell.

London Business Angels

Location: London
Currency: GBP
Size: 50m
Coverage: National
Bio: Connects innovating fast growth technology companies to equity finance through their membership of experienced angel investors.
Investment: 150k - 3m
Website: www.lbangels.co.uk
Contact email: investors@lbangels.co.uk
Contact tel: +44 2073215672

Martlet

Currency: GBP
Size: 1bn
Coverage: National
Bio: Sectors considered: Most B2B Sectors. ICT, medtech, clean tech, energy.
Investment: 150 - 250k
Business Type/Stage: Start-ups, Early Stage
Website: www.martlet-angel.com

Minerva Business Angel Network

Location: Coventry
Coverage: National
Bio: Stimulates the growth of innovation-led businesses in any commercial sector.
Investment: 50k - 1m
Website: www.minerva.uk.net
Contact tel: +44 247632312

MMC Ventures

Currency: GBP
Size: 10m
Coverage: National
Bio: Sectors considered: Financial services, business services, business software, digital media, e-commerce
Investment: 500k - 3m
Website: www.mmcventures.com
Contact tel: +44 2079382220

MoreThanAngels Ltd

Coverage: National
Bio: Their expertise is drawn from considerable experience and proven track records of running and investing in food businesses.
Investment: 150 - 500k
Business Type/Stage: All stages. SMEs
Website: www.morethanangels.com
Contact email: brian@morethanangels.com

MSC R&D

Location: Sheffield
Currency: GBP

Size: 180m
Coverage: National
Bio: Provides a range of strategic, integrated R&D funding and business growth services.
Website: www.mscrnd.com
Contact email: iaingray@mscbdg.co.uk
Contact tel: +44 1142308401

Nesta

Location: London
Currency: GBP
Size: 50m
Coverage: National
Bio: Independent charity providing investments and grants and mobilising research, networks and skills.
Business Type/Stage: Technology Start-ups
Website: www.nesta.org.uk
Contact email: information@nesta.org.uk
Contact tel: +44 2074382500

North Invest

Location: Leeds
Coverage: North England
Bio: Promote equitable investment in the North of the UK.
Investment: 150 - 500k
Website: www.northinvest.co.uk
Contact email: web.enquiries@northinvest.co.uk

Northstar Ventures

Location: Newcastle
Currency: GBP
Size: 80m
Coverage: North East England
Bio: Technology investments.
Investment: 50 - 750k
Business Type/Stage: Early Stage
Website: www.northstarventures.co.uk
Contact tel: +44 1912292770

Northwest Business Angels

Location: Manchester
Coverage: North West
Bio: Provide opportunities for investment in some of the Northwest businesses with growth potential.
Investment: 150 - 500k
Website: www.nwbusinessangels.co.uk
Contact tel: +44 1613593050

Octopus Investments

Location: London
Currency: GBP
Size: 5.5bn
Coverage: National
Bio: Looking for unusually talented teams intent on building businesses that can scale explosively to create, transform or dominate an industry.
Investment: 250k - 3m
Website: www.octopusinvestments.com
Contact tel: +44 8003162295

Oxford Investment Opportunity Network Limited (OION)

Location: Oxford
Currency: GBP
Size: 50m
Coverage: National
Bio: OION is made up of three trading names OION, Thames Valley Investment Network (TVIN) and Oxford Early Investments (OEI). OION is FCA regulated with active investors interested in sectors and stage of business that covers patent rich and technology focused early stage companies. Additionally OION has an (S)EIS fund that invests in some of the companies that are presented to its angels.
Investment: 200k -1.5m
Business Type/Stage: Early Stage
Website: www.oion.co.uk
Contact email: contact@oion.co.uk
Contact tel: +44 (0)1865261480

Origin Capital
Coverage: National
Bio: Most sectors considered; particularly keen on technology (wide definition). All equity and debt structures considered.
Investment: 150 - 500k
Business Type/Stage: Early Stage
Website: www.origingroup.co.uk
Contact email: info@origingroup.co.uk

PHD Equity Partners LLP
Location: Warrington
Coverage: National
Bio: Manages one of the UK's largest private equity funds exclusively funded by private investors.
Investment: 150k - 1m
Website: www.phdequitypartners.com
Contact email: andy@phdequitypartners.com

Portfolio Ventures
Coverage: National, International
Bio: Works with companies across sectors that have a proven business model with early revenues and are in a position to scale.
Investment: 250k - 3m
Business Type/Stage: Early Stage
Website: www.portfolio.ventures
Contact email: hello@portfolio.ventures
Contact tel: +44 7779223837

PwC
Location: New York
Currency: USD
Size: 35bn
Coverage: National
Bio: Advisor for private businesses and private clients
Business Type/Stage: Start, Growth, Expand
Website: www.pwc.co.uk
Contact tel: +44 2075835000

Qi3 Accelerator

Coverage: National
Bio: Sectors considered: manufacturing, engineering, software, healthcare and cleantech
Investment: 150k - 1m
Business Type/Stage: Early Stage
Website: www.qi3.co.uk
Contact tel: +44 1223422404

Ranworth Capital Limited

Location: West Sussex
Coverage: National
Bio: Most sectors considered including EIS/SEIS qualifying.
Investment: 150k - 3m
Business Type/Stage: Start, Growth, Expand, SMEs
Website: www.ranworthcapital.com
Contact tel: +44 1342778000

Rockstar Hubs

Coverage: London
Bio: Sectors considered: Any sector that has proven marked sales and a desire to invest into China.
Investment: 150 - 500k
Business Type/Stage: SMEs
Website: www.rockstarhubs.com
Contact tel: +44 2037518150

Roundcape Ltd

Location: London
Coverage: National, European
Bio: Helps companies by complementing their teams on key functions, such as fundraising, strategy, business development, and operations.
Business Type/Stage: Start-ups
Website: www.roundcape.com
Contact email: info@roundcape.com
Contact tel: +44 2032891891

Royal Society Enterprise Fund

Location: London
Coverage: National
Bio: Sectors considered: Outstanding science & technology
Investment: 150k - 1m
Business Type/Stage: Start-ups
Website: www.royalsociety.org
Contact tel: +44 2074512500

Ruffena Capital

Coverage: National, European
Bio: Opens doors to bring investors the best in alternative, residual and high-growth unquoted investment and financing options.
Investment: 250k - 3m
Website: www.ruffena.co.uk
Contact email: team@ruffena.com
Contact tel: +44 845791086

Seedrs Limited

Coverage: National
Bio: Online platform for investing. They allow qualified investors from all backgrounds and at all levels of wealth to invest.
Investment: 10 - 150k
Business Type/Stage: Start-ups
Website: www.seedrs.com
Contact email: support@seedrs.com

Seraphim Capital

Location: London
Currency: GBP
Size: 30m
Coverage: National
Bio: The fund's primary focus is on UK-centric companies looking for equity capital.
Investment: 0.5 - 2m
Website: www.seraphimcapital.co.uk
Contact email: info@seraphimcapital.co.uk
Contact tel: +44 2036742805

Shawbrook

Bio: Specialist asset-based lender, focused on delivering event-driven transactions to companies with revenues of more than £1m.
Investment: 25m
Website: www.shawbrook.co.uk
Contact email: secured@shawbrook.co.uk
Contact tel: +44 3456506287

Smedvig Capital

Location: London
Currency: GBP
Coverage: UK and the Nordics
Bio: Smedvig Capital is a London based growth capital investor. They are now investing their 14th fund, having deployed more than $800M over the last 20+ years in Series A and Series B funding rounds. They are passionate about finding and supporting the best tech enabled businesses in the UK and Nordics.
Investment: 2 - 15m
Website: www.smedvigcapital.com
Contact email: enquiries@smedvigcapital.com
Contact tel: +44 2074512100

Space Angels Network

Bio: Investors focused specifically on aerospace ventures.
Investment: 150k - 1m
Business Type/Stage: Early Stage
Website: www.spaceangels.com

Startup2Venture

Location: London
Website: startup2venture.wordpress.com
Contact email: startup2venture@gmail.com

Summit Group

Location: London
Coverage: National
Bio: Invests in businesses, providing finance, business relationships, management and administrative support to help them grow.
Investment: 150 - 500k

Business Type/Stage: Early Stage
Website: www.summit-group.co.uk
Contact email: info@summit-group.co.uk

Surrey 100 Club
Location: Surrey
Coverage: National
Bio: Coaches entrepreneurial startups and brings together angel investors and high quality, high potential start-up businesses from Surrey Incubation, the world renowned SETsquared Partnership and more widely across the UK.
Business Type/Stage: Early Stage
Website: www.surrey100club.co.uk
Contact tel: +44 1483682682

Surrey Incubation
Location: Surrey
Coverage: South East
Bio: Provides exceptional business support for entrepreneurs with high-tech start-ups that have the potential for high growth.
Business Type/Stage: Start-ups
Website: www.surreyincubation.co.uk

SyndicateRoom
Coverage: National
Bio: Equity crowd funding platform that allows the crowd to invest in real angel investments by co-investing with seasoned angel investors.
Investment: 150k - 3m
Website: www.syndicateroom.com
Contact email: contactus@syndicateroom.com
Contact tel: +44 1223478558

TBAT Innovation
Location: Derbyshire
Coverage: National
Bio: Specialises in assisting its clients to access funds through numerous sources.
Website: www.tbat.co.uk

Techstars

Location: London
Coverage: National, European, International
Bio: Mentorship driven investment programme. Technology sectors considered.
Investment: 15k
Business Type/Stage: Seed Stage
Website: www.techstars.com

UK Business Angels Association

Location: London
Bio: The national trade association representing angel and early stage investment in the UK. UKBAA connects all those involved in the angel investment market.
Business Type/Stage: Early Stage
Website: www.ukbusinessangelsassociation.org.uk
Contact email: info@ukbusinessangelsassociation.org.uk

Venture Founders

Coverage: National
Bio: UK-based equity crowdfunding platform with a wealth of investment. EIS eligible.
Investment: 150k - 3m
Business Type/Stage: Start-ups
Website: www.venturefounders.co.uk
Contact email: info@venturefounders.co.uk
Contact tel: +44 2036916370

VN Capital Partners

Coverage: National
Bio: Specialise in finding, qualifying, funding, developing, delivering and commercialising renewable energy solutions from 'Idea to Concept'.
Investment: 150 - 250k
Website: www.vn-cp.co.uk
Contact email: info@vn-cp.co.uk
Contact tel: +44 2079935307

Wild Blue Cohort

Location: London
Coverage: London
Bio: Sectors considered: All, particularly SEIS and EIS

Investment: 150k - 1m
Business Type/Stage: Start-ups
Contact email: david@wildbluekc.com
Contact tel: +44 7775945302

WK Capital LLP
Location: London
Coverage: National
Bio: Investment and advice for individuals seeking to build a bespoke portfolio of investment in small, growing UK based private companies of at least £500,000.
Investment: 500k - 3m
Business Type/Stage: Growth Stage
Contact tel: +44 2074031877

Wren Capital
Coverage: National
Bio: Sectors considered: healthcare, energy, food & drink, and high-tech engineering
Investment: 150 - 250k
Business Type/Stage: Early Stage
Website: www.wrencapital.co.uk
Contact tel: +44 2033973390

Xenos
Location: Cardiff
Currency: GBP
Size: 20m
Coverage: Wales
Bio: Mentors and introduces investors to companies seeking growth funding. In return, the company offers an equity share in the business.
Investment: 150 - 500k
Business Type/Stage: Growth Stage
Website: www.xenos.co.uk
Contact tel: +44 2920338144

Zeus Capital
Location: London
Currency: GBP

Size: 1.2bn

Coverage: National

Bio: Zeus Capital is an independent investment banking boutique, providing the highest quality advice to clients across a range of sectors and transactions.

Investment: 150k - 3m

Business Type/Stage: Early Stage

Website: www.zeuscapital.co.uk

Contact email: info@zeuscapital.co.uk

Contact tel: +44 2038295000

2.4

US VENTURE CAPITAL INVESTORS

500 Startups
Location: Mountain View
Currency: USD
Size: 125m
Targeting: Asia, Europe, India, Japan, United States
Bio: Commercial services, software
Investment: 100 - 200k
Portfolio: mClinica, Airseed, EVENTup
Stage: Early Stage
Website: www.500.co

5AM Ventures
Location: Menlo Park
Currency: USD
Size: 685m
Targeting: USA
Bio: Pharmaceuticals and biotechnology
Portfolio: Audentes Therapeutics, EPIRUS Biopharmaceuticals, Cidara Therapeutics

Stage: Early Stage
Website: www.5amventures.com
Contact email: info@5amventures.com
Contact tel: +1 6502338600

Abingworth
Location: London, Menlo Park, Boston
Currency: USD
Size: 375m
Targeting: Europe and USA
Bio: Dedicated exclusively to the life sciences and healthcare sectors. Focus primarily on private companies but are able to invest a percentage of their value in public companies.
Investment: 15 - 30m
Portfolio: Xenogen, Iconix, Ablynx +
Stage: Early, Mid & Late Stage
Website: www.abingworth.com
Contact tel: +44 2075341500

Accel Partners
Location: Palo Alto, Silicon Valley, New York, Bangalore, London
Currency: USD
Size: 17bn
Targeting: Worldwide
Bio: Invest into what they call 'category-defining technology companies'. Consumer internet, digital media, mobile.
Investment: 500k - 50m
Portfolio: Spotify, Lynda, Etsy +
Stage: Late Stage
Website: www.accel.com
Contact tel: +44 2071701000

Advanced Technology Ventures
Location: Menlo Park
Currency: USD
Size: 703m
Targeting: USA

Bio: Bi-coastal venture capital firm that focuses on communications, infrastructure, software and services, consumer technology, biopharmaceuticals, medical devices and cleantech.
Portfolio: Aquion Energy, GluMetrics +
Website: www.atvcapital.com
Contact tel: +1 6503218601

Advantage Capital
Location: USA
Currency: USD
Size: 1.9bn
Targeting: USA
Bio: Invests in a range of industries, including the communication, information technology, life science, business services, manufacturing and energy sectors.
Investment: 500k - 10m
Portfolio: 500k - 10m
Stage: Late Stage
Website: www.advantagecap.com
Contact tel: +1 2568838711

Aisling Capital
Location: New York City
Currency: USD
Size: 1.6bn
Bio: Pharmaceuticals and biotechnology
Portfolio: Syros Pharmaceuticals, Cidara Therapeutics, Loxo Oncology
Stage: Early Stage
Website: www.aislingcapital.com
Contact tel: +1 2126516380

Alexandria Venture
Location: Pasadena, CA
Targeting: USA
Bio: Pharmaceuticals and biotechnology
Portfolio: Syros Pharmaceuticals, Indi Molecular, Visterra
Stage: Early Stage
Website: www.are.com
Contact email: corporateinformation@are.com
Contact tel: +1 6265780777

AME Cloud Ventures
Location: Palo Alto
Currency: USD
Bio: Software
Portfolio: BitPay, Altiscale, Hampton Creek Foods
Stage: Early Stage
Website: www.amecloudventures.com

Andreessen Horowitz
Location: Menlo Park
Currency: USD
Targeting: USA
Bio: Consumer products and services, software
Portfolio: Zenefits Insurance Service, Optimizely, CipherCloud +
Stage: Early Stage
Website: www.a16z.com
Contact email: businessplans@a16z.com

ARCH Venture Partners
Location: Chicago
Currency: USD
Size: 1.6bn
Targeting: USA
Bio: Commercial services, healthcare devices and supplies, pharmaceuticals and biotechnology
Portfolio: Blackthorn Therapeutics, Juno Therapeutics +
Stage: Early Stage
Website: www.archventure.com
Contact email: Inquiries@ARCHVenture.com
Contact tel: +1 7733806600

Atlas Ventures
Location: Massachusetts
Currency: USD
Size: 1.8bn
Targeting: Worldwide
Bio: Invests at the earliest stages in technology and life-sciences companies.
Investment: 500k - 5m

Portfolio: Zoopla, Seatwave +
Stage: Early & Mid Stage
Website: www.atlasventure.com
Contact tel: +1 8572012700

Bain Capital Ventures
Location: Boston, New York, San Francisco, Palo Alto
Currency: USD
Size: 3bn
Targeting: Worldwide
Bio: Focused on high-growth enterprise software opportunities across functions and industries, including Infrastructure Software, SaaS and data services, marketing tech, fintech and healthcare.
Investment: 1m
Portfolio: Accelerate, LinkedIn +
Stage: Early Stage
Website: www.baincapitalventures.com
Contact email: BCV@baincapitalventures.com
Contact tel: +1 6175162000

Battery Ventures
Location: Boston
Currency: USD
Size: 4.7bn
Bio: Commercial services, communications and networking, semiconductors, software
Portfolio: HomeSuite, Tomfoolery
Stage: Early Stage
Website: www.battery.com
Contact tel: +1 6179483600

BBVA Ventures
Location: Madrid, San Francisco
Currency: USD
Size: 100m
Targeting: USA, EU
Bio: BBVA Ventures provides funding and expertise to promising technology companies disrupting financial services.

Portfolio: Prosper, DocuSign, Simple, Radius, Coinbase, SumUp, Personal Capital and Ribbit Capital +
Stage: Early, Mid & Late Stage
Website: www.bbvaventures.com

BDMI
Location: Berlin, New York
Currency: EUR
Size: 16bn
Targeting: North America, Europe, Israel
Bio: Digital Media
Investment: 0.5 - 4m
Portfolio: Seedcamp, Dealvertise +
Stage: Early Stage
Website: www.bdmifund.com
Contact email: info@bdmifund.com
Contact tel: +49 30747844096

Benchmark Capital
Location: Woodside, CA
Currency: USD
Size: 500m
Targeting: Europe, USA
Bio: Communications and networking, media, software
Portfolio: Tinder, Vessel, Optimizely
Stage: Early Stage
Website: www.benchmark.com
Contact email: informationus@benchmark.com

Bessemer Venture Partners
Location: Larchmont, New York
Currency: USD
Size: 4bn
Targeting: Americas, Brazil, Europe, Middle East, United States
Bio: Investment focus on entrepreneurial companies in healthcare, information systems, telecommunications and retailing.
Portfolio: Flex Pharma, Stratoscale, PagerDuty
Website: www.bvp.com

Contact email: businessplan@bvp.com
Contact tel: +1 9148339100

Bezos Expeditions
Location: Mercer Island
Currency: USD
Size: 1bn
Targeting: USA
Bio: Software
Portfolio: Juno Therapeutics, Vessel +
Stage: Early Stage
Website: www.bezosexpeditions.com
Contact email: info@bezosexpeditions.com

Bloomberg Beta
Location: New York City
Currency: USD
Size: 75m
Website: www.github.com

BlueRun Ventures
Location: Menlo Park
Currency: USD
Size: 775m
Targeting: USA, China, South Korea
Bio: Mobile, fintech, commerce, Big Data
Portfolio: BRV-V, BRV Lotus, BRV Aster
Stage: Early Stage
Website: www.brv.com
Contact tel: +1 6504627250

BP Ventures
Location: Cincinnati, Ohio
Currency: USD
Size: 230m
Targeting: Worldwide
Bio: Invests in private, high growth, disruptive technology companies, accelerating cutting edge innovations that are applicable to the energy sector.

Stage: Start-ups
Website: www.bp.com
Contact email: careline@bp.com

Brentwood Associates
Location: Los Angeles
Currency: USD
Size: 688m
Bio: Investments in growing businesses such as: branded consumer products, consumer and business services, direct marketing, including direct mail and e-commerce, education, health and wellness, restaurants and specialty retail.
Stage: Late Stage
Website: www.brentwood.com
Contact email: info@brentwood.com
Contact tel: +1 3104776611

Canaan Partners
Location: Menlo Park
Currency: USD
Size: 4bn
Targeting: India, Middle East, USA
Bio: Healthcare devices and supplies, pharmaceuticals and biotechnology, semiconductors, software
Portfolio: Syros Pharmaceuticals, Visterra, Navitor Pharmaceuticals
Stage: Early Stage
Website: www.canaan.com
Contact email: idea@canaan.com
Contact tel: +1 6508548092

Canvas Venture Fund
Location: Menlo Park
Currency: USD
Size: 175m
Bio: Financial services, digital health, enterprise SaaS, marketplaces, Big Data, Machine Learning
Portfolio: Viewics, Eden, Transfix, and Zola
Stage: Early Stage
Website: www.canvas.vc
Contact tel: +1 6503887600

Charles River Ventures
Location: Cambridge, Mass.
Currency: USD
Size: 2bn
Bio: Commercial services, communications and networking, computer hardware, IT services, software
Portfolio: Udacity, Symphony Commerce, DoorDash
Stage: Early Stage
Website: www.crv.com
Contact tel: +1 6506875600

Cisco Investments
Location: San Jose, Cal.
Currency: USD
Size: 2bn
Targeting: Canada, China, Europe, India, Middle East, USA
Bio: Software
Portfolio: Covacsis Technologies, Platfora, Stratoscale
Stage: Early Stage
Website: www.ciscoinvestments.com

Clearstone Venture Partners
Location: Santa Monica
Targeting: USA
Bio: Internet, consumer, communications, software
Portfolio: PayPal, BillDesk, rubicon
Website: www.clearstone.com
Contact email: info@clearstone.com

Collaborative Fund
Location: Brooklyn
Currency: USD
Size: 41m
Targeting: Canada, USA
Bio: Software
Portfolio: Drip.fm, Hampton Creek Foods, Fundrise
Stage: Early Stage
Website: www.collaborativefund.com

Comcast Ventures

Location: San Francisco
Targeting: USA
Bio: Software
Portfolio: BirchBox, FlightCar, Hired
Stage: Early Stage
Website: www.comcastventures.com

Connecticut Innovations

Location: Rocky Hill
Currency: USD
Size: 4m
Targeting: USA
Bio: Biotechnology, software, mobile
Investment: 500k - 1m
Stage: Seed, Early & Late
Website: www.ctinnovations.com
Contact tel: +1 8605635851

Correlation Ventures

Location: San Diego
Currency: USD
Size: 194m
Targeting: USA
Bio: Software
Portfolio: Good Eggs, Splice Machine, Gild
Stage: Early Stage
Website: www.correlationvc.com
Contact tel: +1 8584128500

Crestline Investors

Location: Forth Worth, Texas
Currency: USD
Size: 7.6bn
Bio: Pharmaceuticals and biotechnology, software
Portfolio: Juno Therapeutics
Stage: Early Stage
Website: www.crestlineinvestors.com

Contact email: hedgefunds@crestlineinc.com
Contact tel: +1 8173397600

Crosslink Capital
Location: San Francisco
Currency: USD
Size: 1.6bn
Targeting: USA
Bio: Enterprise software, e-commerce, advertising
Portfolio: Pandora, Ancestry.com, Omniture
Stage: Seed, Early & Late
Website: www.crosslinkcapital.com
Contact tel: +1 4156171800

CrunchFund
Location: San Francisco
Currency: USD
Size: 59m
Targeting: Europe, USA
Bio: Software
Portfolio: DigitalOcean, URX, Layer
Stage: Early Stage
Website: www.crunchfund.com
Contact email: crunchfund@gmail.com

DAG Ventures
Location: Palo Alto
Currency: USD
Size: 1.3bn
Targeting: USA
Bio: Energy, information technology, life sciences
Portfolio: Nextdoor, Yelp, Chegg
Stage: Mid Stage
Website: www.dagventures.com
Contact email: info@dagventures.com
Contact tel: +1 6505438180

Data Collective

Location: Data Collective
Currency: USD
Size: 35m
Bio: Software
Portfolio: Clusterk, DoxIQ, Omniome
Stage: Early Stage
Website: www.dcvc.com
Contact email: info@dcvc.com

DCM Ventures

Location: Menlo Park
Currency: USD
Size: 2.5bn
Targeting: China, Japan, USA
Bio: Communications and networking, media, financial services, software
Portfolio: Huodongxing, Zhuo Yi's Beijing Chang Technology Co., Yik Yak
Stage: Early Stage
Website: www.dcm.com
Contact email: businessplan@dcm.com
Contact tel: +1 6502331400

Deerfield Management

Location: New York City
Currency: USD
Size: 4bn
Bio: Healthcare devices and supplies, pharmaceuticals and biotechnology
Portfolio: SHINE Medical Technologies, Audentes Therapeutics, N30 Pharmaceuticals
Stage: Early Stage
Website: www.deerfield.com
Contact email: Karenh@deerfield.com
Contact tel: +1 2125511600

Dorm Room Fund

Location: Philadelphia
Targeting: Worldwide
Bio: Collaborative consumption, finance, sales and marketing, SaaS
Investment: 10 - 100k

Stage: Seed
Website: www.dormroomfund.com

Draper Fisher Jurveston
Location: Menlo Park
Currency: USD
Size: 3.1bn
Targeting: Asia, USA
Bio: Commercial services, communications and networking, media, software
Portfolio: Human Longevity, Shift Technologies, Kiwi
Stage: Early Stage
Website: www.dfj.com
Contact email: press@dfj.com
Contact tel: +1 6502339000

Dundee Venture Capital
Location: Omaha
Currency: USD
Size: 20m
Targeting: Mid West
Bio: Software, mobile, e-commerce
Investment: 50k to 1m
Portfolio: Abodo, HuntForce
Website: www.dundeeventurecapital.com

E.ventures
Location: San Francisco, Berlin
Currency: USD
Size: 130m
Targeting: Worldwide
Bio: Global venture capital firm backing internet and software founders.
Investment: 100k - 10m
Portfolio: CityDeal, KaufDA, Farfetch.com +
Stage: Early Stage
Website: www.eventures.vc
Contact email: info@eventures.vc
Contact tel: +1 4158695200

Elevation Partners

Location: Menlo Park
Bio: Investments in new media and technology businesses.
Portfolio: Palm, Yelp
Website: www.elevation.com
Contact email: info@elevation.com
Contact tel: +1 6506876700

European Founders Fund

Location: Germany
Targeting: Europe, Germany
Bio: Invests in technology companies especially with an internet, software or wireless focus.
Stage: Early & Later.
Website: www.rocket-internet.com
Contact email: investorrelations@rocket-internet.com

Expansion Venture Capital

Location: New York City
Bio: Consumer, mobile, marketplaces, collaborative consumption, auto/transportation, fintech, B2B, SaaS, BigData, real estate, EdTech, e-commerce, gaming.
Stage: Early & Growth Stage
Website: www.expansionvc.com
Contact email: info@expansionvc.com
Contact tel: +1 2122651220

Felicis Ventures

Location: Palo Alto
Currency: USD
Size: 220m
Targeting: Brazil, Canada, Estonia, Finland, Germany, Middle East, USA
Bio: Apparel and accessories, capital markets/institutions, commercial products commercial services, communications and networking, computer hardware, consumer
Investment: 100k - 2m
Portfolio: Vicarious FPC, BitPay, Twice
Stage: Early Stage
Website: www.felicis.com

ff Venture Capital
Location: New York City
Currency: USD
Size: 92m
Targeting: Canada, Middle East, UK, USA
Bio: Commercial services, software
Investment: 50k - 1m
Portfolio: Rinse, Surf Airlines, Ionic Security
Stage: Early Stage
Website: www.ffvc.com/

Fidelity Biosciences
Location: Cambridge, Mass.
Currency: USD
Size: 2tr
Targeting: 2tr
Bio: Pharmaceuticals and biotechnology, software
Portfolio: Coherus Biosciences, Surface Oncology, Dimension Therapeutics
Stage: Early Stage
Website: www.fprimecapital.com
Contact email: info@fprimecapital.com
Contact tel: +1 6172312400

First Round Capital
Location: San Francisco
Currency: USD
Size: 633m
Targeting: USA
Bio: Commercial services, software
Portfolio: Augury, Better Finance, Zendrive +
Stage: Early Stage
Website: www.firstround.com

FirstMark Capital
Location: New York City
Currency: USD
Size: 1.7bn
Targeting: USA

Bio: Software
Portfolio: Symphony Commerce, InVisionApp, ROLI
Stage: Early Stage
Website: www.firstmarkcap.com
Contact email: info@firstmarkcap.com

Flagship Ventures
Location: Cambridge, Mass
Currency: USD
Size: 900m
Targeting: California, Canada, USA
Bio: Pharmaceuticals and biotechnology, software
Investment: 500k - 10m
Portfolio: Moderna Therapeutics, Syros Pharmaceuticals, Visterra
Stage: Early Stage
Website: www.flagshipventures.com
Contact tel: +1 6178681888

Floodgate Fund
Location: Palo Alto
Currency: USD
Size: 265m
Targeting: USA
Bio: Software
Portfolio: Codified, Pantheon, Chloe and Isabel
Stage: Early Stage
Website: www.floodgate.com
Contact email: investors@floodgate.com.
Contact tel: +1 6502047990

Flybridge Capital Partners
Location: Boston
Currency: USD
Size: 560m
Bio: Biotechnology, health care, hardware + software
Stage: Early Stage
Website: www.flybridge.com
Contact email: hello@flybridge.com
Contact tel: +1 6173079292

Forerunner Ventures
Location: San Francisco
Currency: USD
Size: 100m
Targeting: USA
Bio: Consumer non-durables, retail, software
Portfolio: Dollar Shave Club, Chloe and Isabel
Stage: Early Stage
Website: www.forerunnerventures.com
Contact email: info@forerunnerventures.com

Formation 8
Location: San Francisco
Currency: USD
Size: 980m
Targeting: USA, Asia
Bio: Software
Portfolio: Collective Health, Leeo, Oscar Health Insurance
Stage: Early Stage
Website: www.formation8.com
Contact email: info@formation8.com

Foundation Capital
Location: Menlo Park
Currency: USD
Size: 2.8bn
Targeting: USA
Bio: Commercial services, communications and networking, computer hardware, media, software
Portfolio: Caliber, Alchemist Accelerator, Beepi
Stage: Early Stage
Website: www.foundationcapital.com
Contact email: info@foundationcap.com
Contact tel: +1 6506140500

Founders Fund
Location: San Francisco
Currency: GBP

Size: 2.3bn
Targeting: USA
Bio: Commercial services, media, financial services, pharmaceuticals and biotechnology, software.
Portfolio: Collective Health, Hampton Creek Foods, Oscar Health Insurance
Stage: Early Stage
Website: www.foundersfund.com

Franklin Square Capital Partners
Location: Philadelphia
Currency: USD
Size: USD 1.1bn AUM
Bio: Apparel and accessories, commercial products, energy services, utilities.
Portfolio: Global Jet Capital
Stage: Early Stage
Website: www.franklinsquare.com
Contact tel: +1 8776288575

Galen Partners
Location: Stamford
Currency: USD
Size: 1bn
Bio: Leading healthcare venture capital firm that focuses on growth equity investments in healthcare technology enabled services.
Investment: 10 - 30m
Portfolio: lifeIMAGE, Sharecare Inc
Stage: Late Stage
Website: www.galen.com
Contact email: info@galen.com
Contact tel: +1 2036536400

General Atlantic
Location: New York, London, Munich, Amsterdam
Targeting: Worldwide
Portfolio: Adyen, Avant and Klarna +
Website: www.generalatlantic.com
Contact tel: +44 2074843200

General Catalyst
Location: Massachusetts
Currency: USD
Size: 2.7bn
Targeting: USA
Bio: Information technology, clean energy, software and new media, Consumer and enterprise software, mobile
Portfolio: Airbnb, BigCommerce, ClassPass +
Stage: Early Stage and Growth
Website: www.generalcatalyst.com
Contact tel: +1 6172347000

GGV Capital
Location: Menlo Park
Currency: USD
Size: 2.2bn
Targeting: Asia, USA
Bio: Communications and networking, pharmaceuticals and biotechnology, software
Portfolio: Petkit, ExaCloud Systems, GrabTaxi Holdings
Stage: Early Stage
Website: www.ggvc.com
Contact tel: +1 6504752150

Gilde Healthcare Partners
Location: Boston, Netherlands
Currency: USD
Size: 200m
Targeting: Europe, USA
Bio: Investor in fast growing healthcare technology and healthcare services companies.
Investment: 20m
Stage: Multiple
Website: www.gildehealthcare.com
Contact email: healthcare@gildehealthcare.com
Contact tel: +31 302192565

Google Ventures
Location: Mountain View
Currency: USD
Size: 2.4bn
Targeting: UK, Europe, USA
Bio: Provide seed, venture, and growth-stage funding to the companies that they deem the best, and not just worthy investments.
Portfolio: TuneIn, Buttercoin, HubSpot +
Stage: Late Stage
Website: www.gv.com

Granite Ventures
Location: San Francisco
Currency: USD
Size: 150m
Bio: Internet, software, and hardware to cleantech, biotech, and healthcare
Investment: 50k - 5m
Stage: Seed, Early Stage
Website: www.granitevc.com
Contact email:info@granitevc.com
Contact tel: +1 4155917700

Greenhill Capital Partners
Location: New York City
Currency: USD
Size: 875m
Targeting: Europe, Australia, Japan, USA
Bio: Consulting, software, curated web
Website: www.greenhill.com
Contact tel: +44 2071987400

Greycroft Partners
Location: New York City
Currency: USD
Size: 600m
Targeting: USA
Bio: Cable service providers, connectivity products, consulting services (B2B), food products, household products, internet retail, legal services (B2B), media

and information services (B2B), information technology, restaurants, hotels and leisure, real estate services (B2C), recreational goods, specialty retail
Portfolio: Scopely, The RealReal, Avi Networks
Stage: Early Stage
Website: www.greycroft.com
Contact tel: +1 2127563508

Greylock Partners
Location: Menlo Park
Currency: USD
Size: 3.9bn
Targeting: Canada, Europe, Middle East, USA
Bio: Healthcare devices and supplies, healthcare services, software
Portfolio: Vessel, Grand Rounds, Avi Networks
Stage: Early Stage
Website: www.greylock.com
Contact email: press@greylock.com

Grotech Ventures
Location: Vienna, Va.
Currency: USD
Size: 225m
Targeting: USA
Bio: Digital media and e-commerce, mobile, cloud and infrastructure software, enterprise software and Big Data Analytics, security technologies, healthcare information technology
Investment: 500k - 5m
Stage: Early Stage and Growth
Website: www.grotech.com
Contact tel: +1 7036379555

H.I.G Capital
Location: Miami FL
Currency: USD
Size: 19bn
Targeting: USA, Europe
Bio: Advertising, biotechnology, wireless
Investment: 5 - 30m

Stage: Seed, Early Stage, Late Stage
Website:www.higcapital.com
Contact email: info@higcapital.com.
Contact tel: +1 3053792322

Harris & Harris Group
Location: New York City
Bio: Semiconductors, biotechnology, clean-tech
Portfolio: Metabolon, Nano Terra
Website: www.hhvc.com
Contact email: admin@hhvc.com
Contact tel: +1 2125820900

Harrison Metal Capital
Location: Palo Alto
Currency: USD
Size: 68m
Targeting: USA
Bio: Software
Portfolio: Grand Rounds, AltSchool, PagerDuty
Stage: Early Stage
Website: www.harrisonmetal.com
Contact email: info@harrisonmetal.com

Hercules Technology Growth Capital
Location: Palo Alto
Currency: USD
Size: 1.3bn
Targeting: USA, Asia, Europe
Bio: Technology, biotechnology, life sciences, healthcare, energy and renewables.
Investment: 5 - 100m
Portfolio: Box, Insmed, kaleo +
Website: www.htgc.com
Contact tel: +1 6502893060

Highland Capital Partners Europe
Location: Geneva, Boston, Palo Alto and Shanghai
Currency: USD

Size: 379m
Targeting: European, global ambition
Bio: Invest in rapidly growing European internet, mobile and software companies that address large market opportunities.
Investment: 10 - 30m
Portfolio: Adjust, eGYM, ShopFully +
Website: www.highlandeurope.com
Contact tel: +41 228177200

Horizon Ventures
Location: Los Altos
Currency: USD
Size: 150m
Targeting: San Francisco Bay
Bio: Communications and Systems, component technologies, healthcare IT, software applications for business.
Investment: 2 - 7m
Website: www.horizonvc.com
Contact tel: +1 6509174100

IA Ventures
Location: New York City
Currency: USD
Size: 155m
Targeting: Europe, USA
Bio: Software.
Portfolio: DigitalOcean, TransferWise, DataRobot
Stage: Early Stage
Website: www.iaventures.com

IDG Ventures
Location: San Francisco
Currency: USD
Size: 3.7bn
Targeting: USA
Bio: Media, enterprise IT and consumer.
Investment: 100 - 500k
Portfolio: Fastly, Crux

Stage: Early Stage
Website: www.idgvusa.com
Contact email: plans@idgventures.com

Ignition Partners
Location: Bellevue, WA
Currency: USD
Size: 1bn
Bio: Software, enterprise software, cloud computing.
Website: www.ignitionpartners.com
Contact email: info@ignitionpartners.com

IllinoisVENTURES
Location: Chicago
Bio: Business IT, communications, consumer, infrastructure.
Website: www.illinoisventures.com
Contact tel: +1 3129969715

Innovation Endeavors
Location: Tel Aviv, Palo Alto
Bio: Partners with start-ups that apply cutting edge technology to transform large industries.
Portfolio: Uber, Quixey +
Stage: Early Stage
Website: www.innovationendeavors.com
Contact email: info@innovationendeavors.com

In-Q-Tel
Location: Arlington, Virginia
Bio: Invests in high-tech companies for the sole purpose of keeping the Central Intelligence Agency.
Website: www.iqt.org
Contact email: info@iqt.org
Contact tel: +1 7032483000

Insight Venture Partners
Location: New York City
Currency: USD
Size: 9.8m

Bio: Media, retail, software
Portfolio: 5Nine software, Wealth-X, Campaign Monitor
Stage: Early Stage
Website: www.insightpartners.com
Contact email: growth@insightpartners.com
Contact tel: +1 2122309200

Institutional Venture Partners
Location: Menlo Park
Currency: USD
Size: 4bn
Targeting: USA
Bio: Commercial services, communications and networking, computer hardware, healthcare devices and supplies, pharmaceuticals and biotechnology, software
Investment: 10 - 100m
Portfolio: Zenefits Insurance Services, ZipRecruiter, ThreatStream
Stage: Early Stage
Website: www.ivp.com
Contact tel: +1 6508540132

Intel Capital
Location: Santa Clara, California
Currency: USD
Size: 1.2bn
Targeting: Worldwide
Bio: Most active VC investor in cybersecurity, hardware, storage, internet of things and wearables.
Portfolio: Swisscom, BP, BBVA
Website: www.intelcapital.com

Intellectual Ventures
Location: Bellevue, WA
Bio: Cleantech, computing, consumer internet, digital home and digital media, manufacturing and memory, mobility, software and services
Website: www.intellectualventures.com
Contact email: info@intven.com
Contact tel: +1 4254672300

Interwest Partners
Location: Menlo Park
Currency: USD
Size: 2.8bn
Targeting: USA
Bio: Computer hardware, healthcare devices and supplies, healthcare services, pharmaceuticals and biotechnology, semiconductors, software
Investment: 7 - 15m
Portfolio: Indi Molecular, Cidara Therapeutics, PMV Pharmaceuticals
Stage: Early Stage
Website: www.interwest.com
Contact tel: +1 6508548585

Iridium Communications
Location: McLean, VA
Bio: Commercial services, transportation
Portfolio: Alreon
Stage: Early Stage
Website: www.iridium.com
Contact email: ken.levy@iridium.com
Contact tel: +1 7032877570

JMI Equity
Location: Baltimore, MD
Currency: USD
Size: 3bn
Targeting: USA
Bio: Software, enterprise software, cloud computing
Portfolio: Twilio, Lyft, eShares
Website: www.jmi.com
Contact tel: +1 4109510200

K9 Ventures
Location: Baltimore
Currency: USD
Size: 46m
Bio: Enterprise software, software, crowdsourcing
Website: www.k9ventures.com

Kapor Capital
Location: Oakland
Bio: Education, mobile, software
Website: www.kaporcapital.com
Contact email: info@kaporcapital.com

Khosla Ventures
Location: Palo Alto
Currency: USD
Size: 3.1bn
Targeting: China, USA
Bio: Cleantech, Mobile, Software
Portfolio: Summonm, Dateram,Tule Technologies +
Stage: Seed, Early & Late
Website: www.khoslaventures.com
Contact email: kv@khoslaventures.com.
Contact tel: +1 6503768500

Kleiner Perkins Caufield Byers
Location: Menlo Park
Currency: USD
Size: 6.8bn
Targeting: China, USA
Bio: Commercial services, computer hardware, healthcare devices and supplies, media, financial services, pharmaceuticals and biotechnology, software
Portfolio: Crossfader, Farmers Edge Precision Consulting, Chill
Stage: Early Stage
Website: www.kpcb.com
Contact email: plans@kpcb.com
Contact tel: +1 6502332750

Laboratory Corporation of America
Location: New York City
Targeting: USA
Bio: Healthcare services
Portfolio: Flatiron Health
Stage: Early Stage
Website: www.labcorp.com

Lerer Hippeau Ventures
Location: New York City
Currency: USD
Size: 131m
Targeting: USA
Bio: Commercial services, software
Portfolio: Augury, Expa Capital, Percolate Industries
Stage: Early Stage
Website: www.lererhippeau.com
Contact email: contact@lererhippeau.com
Contact tel: +1 6462374837

Lightspeed Venture Partners
Location: Menlo Park
Currency: GBP
Size: 3.7bn
Targeting: Europe, Middle East, USA
Bio: Information technology
Portfolio: Little Things, Affirm, Elementum +
Stage: Early Stage
Website: www.lsvp.com
Contact email: info@lsvp.com
Contact tel: +1 6502348300

M/C Venture Partners
Location: Boston
Currency: USD
Size: 176m
Targeting: Canada, USA, Europe
Bio: Mobile, software, enterprise software
Investment: 5 - 50m
Stage: Early, Mid, Late Stage
Website: www.mcpartners.com
Contact email: mcp@mcpartners.com
Contact tel: +1 6173457200

Madrona Venture Group
Location: Seattle
Currency: USD

Size: 967m
Targeting: USA
Bio: Retail, software
Portfolio: Spare5, Igneous Systems, Context Relevant
Stage: Early Stage
Website: www.madrona.com
Contact tel: +1 2066743000

Matrix Partners
Location: Palo Alto
Currency: USD
Size: 1.7bn
Targeting: USA
Bio: software, enterprise software, mobile, fintech, SaaS, e-commerce
Portfolio: Oculus VR, Zendesk, HubSpot, JustFab +
Stage: Early Stage
Website: www.matrixpartners.com
Contact email: info@matrixpartners.com
Contact tel: +1 6507981600

Maveron
Location: San Francisco
Currency: USD
Size: 780m
Targeting: USA
Bio: E-commerce, curated web, education
Portfolio: eBay, Capella Education +
Stage: Early, Mid and Late Stage
Website: www.maveron.com
Contact tel: +1 4153736250

Menlo Ventures
Location: Menlo Park
Currency: USD
Size: 4bn
Targeting: USA
Bio: Communications and networking, computer hardware, healthcare devices and supplies, software

Portfolio: PernixData, Avi Networks, Munchery
Stage: Early Stage
Website: www.menlovc.com
Contact tel: +1 6508548540

Meritech Capital Partners
Location: Palo Alto
Currency: USD
Size: 1.26bn
Targeting: USA
Bio: Software, social media, security, enterprise software, medical devices, fintech
Investment: 10 - 50m
Stage: Later Stage
Website: www.meritechcapital.com
Contact email: info@meritechcapital.com
Contact tel: +1 6504752200

Merus Capital
Location: Palo Alto
Currency: USD
Size: 90m
Bio: Software, internet, SaaS
Website: www.meruscap.com
Contact email: info@meruscap.com

Moduslink Global Solutions
Location: Delaware
Currency: USD
Size: 754m
Targeting: North America, Europe and Asia
Bio: Provides supply chain management services to global technology and software companies across its worldwide operations.
Website: www.moduslink.com
Contact tel: +1 7816635000

Morgenthaler
Location: Menlo Park
Currency: USD
Size: 1.25bn

Targeting: Asia, Canada, USA, Europe
Bio: Biotechnology, healthcare, software
Investment: 5 – 15m
Stage: Early & Late
Website: www.morgenthaler.com
Contact email: hlagrone@morgenthaler.com
Contact tel: +1 6503883676

Mousse Partners

Location: New York City
Targeting: USA
Bio: Consumer products and services
Portfolio: SeatGeek, Epirus Biopharmaceuticals, Spire
Stage: Early Stage
Contact tel: +1 2123035795

MPM Capital

Location: Boston
Currency: USD
Size: 2.1m
Targeting: Africa, Americas, Asia, Canada, Europe, Middle East, Oceania, USA
Bio: Healthcare devices and supplies, pharmaceuticals and biotechnology
Portfolio: Mitokyne, Raze Therapeutics, True North Therapeutics
Stage: Early Stage
Website: www.mpmcapital.com
Contact email: info@mpmcapital.com

New Enterprise Associates

Location: Menlo Park
Currency: USD
Size: 13bn
Targeting: Asia, Brazil, USA
Bio: Communications and networking, energy services, exploration, production and refining, healthcare devices and supplies, IT services, pharmaceuticals and biotechnology, software.
Portfolio: FIRE1, Jet, Lumena Pharmaceuticals +
Stage: Early Stage
Website: www.nea.com
Contact tel: +1 6508549499

NextView Ventures
Location: Boston
Currency: USD
Size: 61m
Targeting: USA
Bio: Analytics, curated web, e-commerce
Investment: 0.25 - 0.5m
Stage: Seed Stage
Website: www.nextviewventures.com

Norwest Venture Partners
Location: Palo Alto
Currency: USD
Size: 5bn
Targeting: India, Middle East, USA
Bio: Communications and networking, computer hardware, software
Portfolio: IFTTT, Kendra Scott, Bitglass
Stage: Early Stage
Website: www.nvp.com
Contact email: bizplan@nvp.com

Oak Investment Partners
Location: Greenwich, CT
Currency: USD
Size: 2.5bn
Targeting: Asia, Canada, Europe, Israel, USA
Bio: Cleantech, software, semiconductors
Investment: 10 - 150m
Stage: Seed, Early & Late Stage
Website: www.oakvc.com
Contact tel: +1 2032268346

OATV (O'Reilly AlphaTech Ventures)
Location: San Francisco
Investment: 10 - 100k
Website: www.oatv.com
Contact tel: +1 4156930200

OCA Ventures
Location: Chicago
Currency: USD
Size: 100m
Targeting: USA
Bio: Software, security, network security
Stage: Seed, Early & Late
Website: www.ocaventures.com
Contact tel: +1 3123278400

OrbiMed Advisors
Location: New York City
Currency: USD
Size: 12bn
Targeting: Americas, Asia, Canada, Europe, Middle East, USA
Bio: Healthcare devices and supplies, pharmaceuticals and biotechnology
Portfolio: Acutus Medical, Audentes Therapeutics, Armo BioSciences
Stage: Early Stage
Website: www.orbimed.com
Contact email: NeildC@OrbiMed.com
Contact tel: +1 2127396400

Pappas Ventures
Location: Durham, NC
Targeting: North America
Bio: Focused exclusively on investing in the life sciences.
Website: www.pappasventures.com
Contact email: jsmith@pappasventures.com.
Contact tel: +1 9199983300

Partech Ventures
Location: Paris, Berlin, San Francisco
Currency: USD
Size: 240m
Targeting: Worldwide
Bio: Technology companies and digital media
Investment: 200k - 50m
Portfolio: Made.com, Qype, Daily Motion +

Stage: Early & Mid Stage
Website: www.partechventures.com
Contact email: sjameau@partechventures.com

Point Judith Capital
Location: Boston
Currency: USD
Size: 12.5bn
Bio: Software, technology enabled services
Investment: 500k - 3m
Website: www.pointjudithcapital.com
Contact email: info@pointjudithcapital.com
Contact tel: +1 6176006260

Polaris Partners
Location: Waltham, Mass
Currency: USD
Size: 3.5bn
Targeting: Europe, USA
Bio: Healthcare devices and supplies, pharmaceuticals and biotechnology, semiconductors, software
Portfolio: Syros Pharmaceuticals, Visterra, Navitor Pharmaceuticals
Stage: Early Stage
Website: www.polarispartners.com
Contact email: partnership@polarispartners.com
Contact tel: +1 8557873500

QED Investors
Location: Alexandria, VA
Bio: Software, automotive insurance, broadcasting, radio and television, business/ productivity software, cable service providers, consumer finance, information services (B2C), Internet service providers, logistics, media and information services (B2B), financial services, publishing, security services (B2B), social/platform software, telecommunications service providers, wireless service providers
Portfolio: Privlo, Remitly
Stage: Early Stage
Website: www.qedinvestors.com

Qualcomm Ventures
Location: San Diego
Currency: USD
Size: 500m
Targeting: Asia, Middle East, USA
Bio: Software
Portfolio: Birds Eye Systems, Cambridge Wowo, Traffline
Stage: Early Stage
Website: www.qualcommventures.com

Quest Venture Partners
Location: Menlo Park
Currency: USD
Size: 45m
Bio: Mobile, advertising, e-commerce
Investment: 10k - 2.5m
Stage: Seed, Early & Late
Website: www.questvp.com

RA Capital Management
Location: Boston
Currency: USD
Size: 391m
Targeting: USA
Bio: Pharmaceuticals and biotechnology, software
Portfolio: Coherus Biosciences, Lumena Pharmaceuticals, N30 Pharmaceuticals
Stage: Early Stage
Website: www.racap.com
Contact email: mcalore@racap.com
Contact tel: +1 6177782500

Radius Ventures
Location: New York City
Bio: Health care, biotechnology, health and wellness
Investment: 10m
Portfolio: Aethon, Tactile
Website: www.radiusventures.com
Contact email: ea@radiusventures.com
Contact tel: +1 2128977778

Redpoint
Location: Menlo Park
Currency: USD
Size: 3.4bn
Targeting: Brazil, China, Europe, Middle East, USA
Bio: Commercial services, communications and networking, retail, software
Portfolio: Beepi, Jaunt, Snowflake Computing
Stage: Early Stage
Website: www.redpoint.com
Contact tel: +1 6509265600

Resolute Ventures
Location: California
Bio: Software, SaaS, analytics
Investment: 50 - 750k
Portfolio: Bitium, GymPact
Stage: Early Stage
Website: www.resolute.vc

Revolution
Location: Washington D.C.
Currency: USD
Size: 658m
Targeting: USA
Bio: Software
Investment: 20m
Portfolio: Handy, Insikt Ventures, OrderUp
Stage: Early Stage
Website: www.revolution.com
Contact tel: +1 2027761400

Rho Ventures
Location: New York City
Currency: USD
Size: 510m
Targeting: USA
Bio: Rho Ventures is a venture capital firm that actively invests in technology, new media, cleantech and healthcare companies.
Investment: 50m

Portfolio: Diversa, iVillage
Stage: Seed, Early & Late
Website: www.rho.com

Rock Springs Capital
Location: Baltimore
Bio: Healthcare devices and supplies, pharmaceuticals and biotechnology
Portfolio: Spark Therapeutics, Coherus Biosciences, N30 Pharmaceuticals
Stage: Early Stage
Website: www.rockspringscapital.com
Contact email: info@rockspringscapital.com

Rockaway Capital
Location: Prague, Sao Paulo, San Francisco
Currency: USD
Size: 253m
Targeting: Worldwide
Bio: Builds the internet economy in emerging markets. Looks for technology Start-ups
Portfolio: SPORTY, SnowBoards, BigBrands +
Stage: Early & Mid Stage
Website: www.rockawaycapital.com
Contact email: info@rockawaycapital.com

Rothenberg Ventures
Location: San Francisco
Currency: USD
Size: 21m
Targeting: USA
Bio: Virtual Reality, Augmented Reality, Robotics, AI, Space, Drones, Next Generation Hardware, IoT
Portfolio: AltspaceVR, Reload, Wevr
Stage: Seed & Early Stage
Website: www.rothenbergventures.com

Route 66 Ventures
Location: Virginia
Targeting: Asia, Europe, Latin America, and Africa
Bio: Financial services and fintech Investment firm.

Investment: 1 - 30m
Portfolio: KNIP, Moven, NextCapital, Payzer, Ripple +
Stage: Early & Growth stage
Website: www.route66ventures.com
Contact tel: +1 7038284198

RRE Ventures

Location: New York City
Currency: USD
Size: 1bn
Targeting: USA
Bio: Financial services, software
Investment: 100k - 25m
Portfolio: Vaurum, Kik Interactive, BitPay
Stage: Early Stage
Website: www.rre.com
Contact email: info@rre.com

Safeguard Scientifics

Location: Radnor, Pennsylvania
Bio: Medical technology, diagnostics, medical devices, healthtech, healthcare IT, digital health, enterprise software, digital media, adtech, fintech
Investment: 5 - 25m
Website: www.safeguard.com
Contact email: Webmaster@safeguard.com
Contact tel: +1 6102930600

Santé Ventures

Location: Austin, TX
Currency: USD
Size: 133m
Targeting: USA
Bio: Biotechnology, health care, health and wellness
Portfolio: BAROnova, Claret Medical
Stage: Early Stage
Website: www.santeventures.com

Saturn Partners

Location: Boston
Targeting: USA
Bio: Looks for companies with potential for significant growth, primarily in information and financial technology, but also in advanced materials and specialty energy.
Investment: 500k - 5m
Stage: Seed & Early Stage
Website: www.saturnpartnersvc.com
Contact email: plans@santeventures.com

SAVP

Location: New York City
Bio: Technology
Investment: 25k - 1m
Portfolio: Critical Mention, Rewind.Me, Knovel
Stage: Early and Growth Stage
Website: www.savp.com
Contact email: partners@savp.com

Sequoia

Location: Menlo Park
Currency: USD
Size: 10bn
Targeting: America, Asia, Europe, Middle East, USA
Bio: Commercial services, communications and networking, pharmaceuticals and biotechnology, restaurants, hotels and leisure, semiconductors, software
Investment: 1 - 100m
Portfolio: Beijing Peak Technology, Daoxlla, Alooma +
Stage: Early Stage
Website: www.sequoiacap.com
Contact tel: +1 6508543927

Shasta Ventures

Location: Menlo Park
Currency: USD
Size: 1bn
Targeting: California
Bio: Software

Portfolio: Delighted, TigerText, Doctor on Demand
Stage: Early Stage
Website: www.shastaventures.com
Contact tel: +1 6505431700

SherpaVentures
Location: San Francisco
Currency: USD
Size: 154m
Bio: Software
Portfolio: Beepi, Expa Capital, Munchery
Stage: Early Stage

Sierra Ventures
Location: San Mateo
Currency: USD
Size: 1.5bn
Targeting: Canada, China, India, USA
Bio: Software, enterprise software, analytics, SaaS, big data, devices, marketplaces
Portfolio: Alpine, Corrigo, Boomtrain
Website: www.sierraventures.com
Contact email: info@sierraventures.com

Sigma + Partners
Location: Boston
Currency: USD
Size: 2bn
Bio: Software, enterprise software, mobile
Website: www.sigmapartners.com
Contact tel: +1 6508531700

Silicon Valley Bank (SVB Capital)
Location: Santa Clara
Currency: USD
Size: 2bn
Targeting: USA, with some global exposure
Bio: Software, technology
Portfolio: Metacloud, Hired, Build.com

Stage: Early Stage
Website: www.svb.com
Contact email: ukclientservice@svb.com

Slow Ventures
Location: Mill Valley, CA
Currency: USD
Size: 75m
Bio: Software
Portfolio: BirchBox, Helium Systems, DineInFresh
Stage: Early Stage
Website: www.slow.co

Social Capital Partnership
Location: Palo Alto
Currency: USD
Size: 550m
Targeting: USA
Bio: Software
Portfolio: Mango Games, Collective Health, Netskope
Stage: Early Stage
Website: www.socialcapital.com
Contact email: inbox@socialcapital.com

Sofinnova Ventures
Location: Menlo Park
Currency: USD
Size: 1bn
Targeting: China, Europe, India, Japan, Middle East, USA
Bio: Communications and networking, healthcare devices and supplies, pharmaceuticals and biotechnology, software
Portfolio: Spark Therapeutics, Coherus Biosciences, Audentes Therapeutics +
Website: www.sofinnova.com
Contact tel: +1 6506818420

Softbank Capital
Location: Newton, Mass
Currency: USD

Size: 23m
Targeting: Asia, USA
Bio: Media, software
Portfolio: FlightCar, NatureBox, Chloe and Isabel
Stage: Early Stage
Website: www.softbank.com
Contact email: ContactUs@SoftBank.com

SoftTech VC
Location: Palo Alto
Currency: USD
Size: 155m
Targeting: USA
Bio: Mobile, Curated Web, Software
Investment: 500k - 1m
Portfolio: August, Clever, DroneDeploy
Stage: Early Stage
Website: www.softtechvc.com

Spark Capital
Location: Boston
Currency: USD
Size: 1.8bn
Targeting: USA
Bio: Media, software, transportation
Portfolio: Skyfi Labs, Privlo, Kik Interactive +
Stage: Early Stage
Website: www.sparkcapital.com

Summit Partners
Location: Boston
Currency: USD
Size: 16bn
Targeting: Americas, Asia, Europe
Bio: Commercial services, communications and networking, healthcare devices and supplies, healthcare services, IT Services, retail, software
Investment: 5 - 500m
Portfolio: City Practice Group Of New York, Gainsight
Stage: Early Stage

Website: www.summitpartners.com
Contact tel: +44 2076597500

SV Angel
Location: Palo Alto
Currency: USD
Size: 104m
Targeting: USA
Bio: Commercial services, software
Portfolio: Delighted, Harry's +
Stage: Early Stage
Website: www.svangel.com

SV Life Sciences Advisers
Location: Boston
Currency: USD
Size: 1.9bn
Targeting: USA, Europe
Bio: Healthcare devices and supplies, pharmaceuticals and biotechnology
Investment: 1 - 40m
Portfolio: Thesan Pharmaceuticals, PanOptica, Spinal Kinetics
Stage: Early Stage
Website: www.svlsa.com
Contact tel: +44 2074217070

T.Rowe Price
Location: Baltimore
Currency: USD
Size: 731bn
Targeting: Asia, USA
Bio: Software
Portfolio: Spark Therapeutics, Diplomat Pharmacy
Stage: Early Stage
Website: www.troweprice.com

TA Associates
Location: London, Boston, Menlo Park, Mumbai and Hong Kong
Currency: USD

Size: 4bn
Targeting: North America, Europe, India, Asia
Bio: Invests in growing private companies in exciting industries including fintech, technology, financial services, healthcare and consumer businesses and communications. Private Equity.
Investment: 50 - 500m
Portfolio: Bats, Creditex +
Stage: Private Equity
Website: www.ta.com
Contact tel: +44 2078230200

Technology Crossover Ventures (TCV)
Location: Palo Alto, Silicon Valley, New York, London
Currency: USD
Size: 9.9bn
Targeting: North America, Europe
Bio: Provides financial, strategic and operational support for today's rapidly growing, innovative tech companies.
Investment: 10 - 100m
Portfolio: Merkle, WorldRemit, Elevate, Think Finance and Trading Screen +
Stage: Early, Late and Private Equity
Website: www.tcv.com
Contact email: ir@tcv.com

Tenaya Capital
Location: Portola Valley
Currency: USD
Size: 1bn
Targeting: USA
Bio: Internet, software, services, fintech, infrastructure
Investment: 5 – 10m
Portfolio: Acquia, Edmodo, Kenshoo
Website: www.tenayacapital.com
Contact tel: +1 6506876500

Third Rock Ventures
Location: Boston
Currency: USD
Size: 1.5m

Targeting: USA
Bio: Pharmaceuticals and biotechnology
Portfolio: PanOptica, Voyager Therapeutics, NinePoint Medical
Stage: Early Stage
Website: www.thirdrockventures.com
Contact tel: +1 6175852000

Thrive Capital
Location: New York City
Currency: USD
Size: 626m
Bio: Consumer non-durables, software
Portfolio: Harry's Razor Company, Oscar Health Insurance, Urban Compass
Stage: Early Stage
Website: www.thrivecap.com
Contact email: info@thrivecap.com

Triangle Peak Partners
Location: Carmel
Currency: USD
Size: 516m
Targeting: USA
Bio: Software
Portfolio: Getaround, Agent Ace +
Stage: Early Stage
Website: www.trianglepeakpartners.com
Contact email: info@trianglepeakpartners.com

True Ventures
Location: Palo Alto
Currency: USD
Size: 905m
Targeting: Europe, USA
Bio: Healthcare technology systems, insurance, software
Portfolio: Crossfader, Ginger.io, ToyTalk
Stage: Early Stage
Website: www.trueventures.com
Contact tel: +1 6503192150

Union Square Ventures
Location: New York City
Currency: USD
Size: 625m
Targeting: USA
Bio: Curated Web, Advertising, Software
Investment: 1 - 20m
Portfolio: Zynga, Twitter and Tumblr.
Website: www.usv.com
Contact tel: +1 2129947880

Valhalla Partners
Location: Vienna, VA
Currency: USD
Size: 260m
Targeting: Mid-Atlantic region of the United States.
Bio: Software, enterprise software, advertising
Stage: Early Stage
Website: www.valhallapartners.com
Contact email: info@valhallapartners.com

VegasTechFund
Location: Las Vegas
Currency: USD
Size: 50m
Targeting: Nevada
Bio: Software
Portfolio: Surf Airlines, OrderWithMe, Banjo
Stage: Early Stage
Website: www.vegastechfund.com

Venrock
Location: Palo Alto
Currency: USD
Size: 2.6m
Targeting: USA
Bio: Communications and networking, pharmaceuticals and biotechnology, software

Portfolio: Juno Therapeutics, Coherus Biosciences +
Stage: Early Stage
Website: www.venrock.com
Contact tel: +1 6505619580

Warburg Pincus

Location: New York
Currency: USD
Size: 37bn
Targeting: Worldwide
Bio: Software, biotechnology, e-commerce
Website: www.warburgpincus.com
Contact tel: +44 2073060377

Wellington Management

Location: Boston
Currency: USD
Size: 927bn
Targeting: USA
Bio: Healthcare devices and supplies, pharmaceuticals and biotechnology
Portfolio: Coupang, Spark Therapeutics, N30 Pharmaceuticals
Stage: Early Stage
Website: www.wellington.com
Contact email: Info@wellington.com

Western Technology Investment

Location: Portola Valley
Currency: USD
Size: 2.3m
Targeting: USA
Bio: Commercial services, communications and networking, computer hardware, software, transportation
Portfolio: Alchemy Web, Beijing Peak Technology, Poynt Co.
Stage: Early Stage
Website: www.westerntech.com
Contact tel: +1 6502344300

Wolverine Venture Fund

Location: Ann Arbor , MI
Currency: USD
Size: 7m
Targeting: USA
Bio: Biotechnology, cleantech, analytics
Investment: 50 - 150k
Portfolio: ArborMetrix, Direct Flow Medical +
Stage: Mid Stage
Website: www.wolverineventurefund.com
Contact email: wvfcontact@umich.edu

WRF Capital

Location: Seattle
Targeting: Washington State
Bio: Pharmaceuticals and biotechnology
Investment: 25k - 1m
Portfolio: Juno Therapeutics, Faraday Pharmaceuticals, SNUPI Technologies
Stage: Early Stage
Website: www.wrfcapital.com
Contact email: info@wrfcapital.com

Y Combinator

Location: Mountain View
Currency: USD
Size: 700m
Bio: Finance, venture capital, consulting, start-ups
Investment: 100 - 200k
Portfolio: Reddit, Heroku and OMGPop
Stage: Early Stage
Website: www.ycombinator.com
Contact email: info@ycombinator.com

2.5

US ANGEL NETWORKS

(GVTA) Great Valley Technology Alliance Angel Network - TecBridge

Location: Pennsylvania

Bio: Technology, entrepreneurship and collaboration, with the purpose of growing technology and biotechnology wealth within Northeastern Pennsylvania.

Business Type/Stage: Early Stage

Website: www.tecbridgepa.org

Contact email: info@tecbridgepa.org

500 Startups

Location: Silicon Valley

Currency: USD

Size: 300m

Investment: 10 - 250k

Business Type/Stage: Early Stage

Website: www.500.co

Acorn Angels

Location: Cupertino

Bio: Early stage investment for high-tech companies.

Business Type/Stage: Early Stage

Website: www.acornangels.com

Contact email: info@AcornAngels.com

Alliance of Angels

Location: Seattle
Currency: USD
Size: 10m
Bio: They invest in a wide range of market sectors, including information technology, consumer products & services, hardware and life sciences.
Investment: 500k - 1.5m
Business Type/Stage: Seed & Early Stage
Website: www.allianceofangels.com
Contact email: aoa@allianceofangels.com

Amidzad Partners

Location: Redwood City
Bio: Invests in emerging growth companies on the West Coast.
Business Type/Stage: Seed & Early Stage
Website: www.amidzad.com
Contact email: marc@amidzad.com

Angel Investor Forum

Location: Connecticut
Bio: AIF members invest their time, talent and money in supporting companies with solid business models and growth potential. By investing together, they provide the capital required ($100k – $2M) with a high return potential.
Investment: 750k - 1.5m
Website: www.angelinvestorforum.com
Contact email: edg@angelinvestorforum.com

AngelsCorner

Location: Silicon Valley
Bio: Focused on investing into private companies with strong teams, proprietary solutions, and high potentials.
Investment: 50k - 3m
Website: www.angelscorner.com

Ann Arbor Angels

Location: Michigan
Bio: Leaders in Michigan's technology business community.
Investment: 100k - 3m

Business Type/Stage: Early Stage
Website: www.annarborangels.org
Contact email: info@annarborangels.org

Ansel Capital Partners

Location: Colorado
Bio: Investment in companies with substantial growth potential but an inability to attract or lack of desire to engage with venture capital.
Investment: 250k - 5m
Business Type/Stage: Seed Stage
Website: www.anselcapitalpartners.com

ARC Angel Fund

Location: New York
Bio: Focus primarily on software, IT, internet, tech-enabled services, business services, digital media, mobile, healthcare IT.
Investment: 100 - 500k
Business Type/Stage: Seed & Early Stage
Website: www.arcangelfund.com

ARCH Development Partners

Location: Illinois
Bio: Focuses on research based technologies including biotechnology/life sciences, wireless software and technology infrastructure.
Business Type/Stage: Seed Stage
Website: www.archdp.com
Contact email: info@archdp.com.com

Ariel Southeast Angel Partners

Location: Georgia
Bio: Member-driven organization composed of experienced business, medical, legal and educational professionals.
Investment: 5k
Business Type/Stage: Early & High Growth
Website: www.arielsoutheastangels.com

Arizona Technology Investor Forum

Location: Arizona

Bio: Bridging the gap between technology start-ups and the nationwide venture capital community.
Website: www.arizonatechinvestors.com
Contact email: jegoulka@atif-az.org

Astia
Location: San Francisco
Bio: Committed to investing in women-led companies.
Investment: 25k
Business Type/Stage: Start up
Website: www.astia.org
Contact email: investors@astia.org.
Contact tel: +1 4154215500

Atlanta Technology Angels
Location: Georgia
Currency: USD
Size: 15m
Bio: Seeks investments in technology companies based in Atlanta.
Investment: 1m
Business Type/Stage: Early Stage
Website: www.angelatlanta.com

Band of Angels
Location: California
Currency: USD
Size: 50m
Bio: Focuses on high technology deals.
Investment: 1 - 1.5m
Business Type/Stage: Seed & Early Stage
Website: www.bandangels.com
Contact email: contactus@bandangels.com

Baseline Ventures
Location: California
Investment: 100 - 300k
Business Type/Stage: Start up
Website: www.baselinev.com
Contact email: steve@baselinev.com

Beacon Angels
Location: Boston, Massachusetts
Bio: Investments in small fast-growing companies.
Investment: 50 - 300k
Website: www.beaconangels.com
Contact email: beacange2@gmail.com

Bellingham Angel Investors
Location: Washington
Business Type/Stage: Seed & Early Stage
Website: www.bellinghamangelinvestors.com
Contact email: jmn@bellinghamangelinvestors.com;
                jj@bellinghamangelinvestors.com

Berkeley Ventures
Location: California
Bio: Focused on helping start-ups in sectors including, but not limited to, internet, software, mobile, clean energy, and gaming.
Business Type/Stage: Start up
Website: www.berkeleyventures.com
Contact email: info@berkeleyventures.com

Bi State Investment Group
Location: Missouri
Business Type/Stage: Early Stage

BioAngels
Location: Illinois
Bio: Invest in medical and life sciences businesses in the Midwest.
Investment: 1m
Business Type/Stage: Startup and Early Stage
Website: www.bioangels.com
Contact email: sborland@bioangels.com

BioCrossroads
Location: Indiana
Currency: USD
Size: 25m

Bio: Invests in biotechnology, pharmaceutical, medical devices, diagnostic, ag-biotech and health information technology
Investment: 1m
Business Type/Stage: Early Stage
Website: www.biocrossroads.com

Bluegrass Angels (BGA)
Location: Kentucky
Business Type/Stage: Start up
Website: www.bluegrassangels.com
Contact email: admin@bluegrassangels.com

BlueTree Allied Angels
Location: Pennsylvania
Business Type/Stage: Early Stage
Website: www.bluetreealliedangels.com
Contact email: info@bluetreecapital.com

Boston Harbor Angels
Location: Massachusetts
Bio: Helps entrepreneurs navigate and grow their businesses through the treacherous waters of an increasingly competitive environment in our global economy.
Investment: 5m
Business Type/Stage: Early Stage
Website: www.bostonharborangels.com

Boston Seed Capital
Location: Massachusetts
Bio: Support for internet-enabled businesses around the country.
Business Type/Stage: Early Stage
Website: www.bostonseed.com

Boynton Angels
Location: Massachusetts
Bio: Invests in technology companies located within a two-hour radius of Worcester, Massachusetts.
Investment: 100 - 500k
Business Type/Stage: Seed and expansion

Website: www.boyntonangels.com
Contact email: info@boyntonangels.com

Bullpen Capital
Location: Menlo Park, California
Bio: Invests in technology companies.
Business Type/Stage: Seed
Website: www.bullpencap.com
Contact email: james@bullpencap.com

Camino Real Angels
Location: El Paso, Texas
Bio: Provide opportunities where their members could realize excellent financial returns by investing in companies located in the Paso del Norte region.
Investment: 2m
Business Type/Stage: Early Stage
Contact email: contactus@caminorealangels.com

Capital Access Network
Location: New York
Bio: Enables entrepreneurs in Maryland, Washington DC, Virginia, and Delaware to connect with active, accredited angel investor.
Business Type/Stage: Start up
Website: www.cancapital.com
Contact tel: +1 8775504731

Capital Community Angels
Location: Michigan
Bio: Helping entrepreneurs of their region succeed and prosper.
Business Type/Stage: Seed and Early Stage
Website: www.ccangels.org
Contact tel: +1 5172420972

Centennial Investors
Location: Missouri
Bio: Created to meet the capital needs of university and private sector entrepreneurs.
Investment: 150 - 500k
Business Type/Stage: Early

Website: www.centennialinvestors.com
Contact tel: +1 5738840496

Central Texas Angel Network
Location: Texas
Currency: USD
Size: 64m
Bio: Provides investment opportunities and assist, educate and connect companies in Central Texas with information and advisors for the purpose of raising money and assisting with their growth.
Business Type/Stage: Early & Growth
Website: www.centraltexasangelnetwork.com
Contact email: director@centraltexasangelnetwork.com

Charleston Angel Partners
Location: South Carolina
Bio: Member-driven organization composed of business professionals working together to help support high growth economic development in the region.
Business Type/Stage: Start up
Website: www.chapsc.com
Contact email: andrea@charlestonangels.com

Cherrystone Angel Group
Location: Rhode Island
Business Type/Stage: Early Stage
Website: www.cherrystoneangelgroup.com
Contact email: info@cherrystoneangelgroup.com

Chesapeake Emerging Opportunities Club
Location: Maryland
Bio: Invests in companies with significant growth potential that operate in large markets and are run by talented management.
Business Type/Stage: Early Stage
Website: www.ceopportunities.com

Chippewa Valley Angel Investor Network
Location: Wisconsin
Bio: Provides a one-stop resource for entrepreneurs seeking equity financing in the Chippewa Valley.

Business Type/Stage: Early Stage
Website: www.momentumwest.org
Contact email: cvangels@execpc.com

Converge Venture Partners
Location: Massachusetts
Bio: Provides capital and communications for tech entrepreneurs.
Business Type/Stage: Seed and Early Stage
Website: www.convergevp.com
Contact email: inquiries@Convergevp.com

Cornerstone Angels
Location: Illinois
Bio: Goal is to help bridge the widening gap between initial start-up capital and institutional financing.
Business Type/Stage: Early Stage
Website: www.cornerstoneangels.com

Curious Office
Location: Washington
Bio: They specialize in design, software development and investment.
Website: www.curiousoffice.com
Contact email: info@curiousoffice.com

DaneVest Capital
Location: Wisconsin
Bio: Creates investment opportunities in privately-held business sectors.
Website: www.danevestcapital.com
Contact email: dvc@danevestcapital.com

Delta Angel Group
Location: Washington
Bio: Not strictly limited to technology-centric companies; companies with significant growth potential and a defensible competitive advantage will be seriously considered.
Business Type/Stage: Early Stage

Delaware Crossing Investor Group
Location: Pennsylvania

Bio: Network of former and current executives and entrepreneurs who provide counsel and capital.
Investment: 250k - 1m
Business Type/Stage: Early & Growth
Website: www.delawarecrossing.org

Desert Angels
Location: Tuscan, Arizona
Bio: The primary focus of the Desert Angels is the funding of entrepreneurial ventures and to that end they review over 100 companies per year as possible investments.
Business Type/Stage: Start up
Website: www.desertangels.org
Contact email: curtis@desertangels.org

Dutchess County Angel Network
Location: New York
Bio: Primary contact for those interested in launching a new business in Dutchess County or relocating an existing business.
Website: www.thinkdutchess.com
Contact tel: +1 8454635400

DWGroup
Location: Chicago
Bio: Invests in international technology, construction and manufacturing sector, building start-up ecosystems, BPO/BPaaS solutions and VC network in Ukraine.
Website: www.deltawebconsulting.com
Contact email: anton.chepurda@deltawebconsulting.com

eCoast Angel Network
Location: New Hampshire
Bio: Focus is on companies involved with advanced technology, e-commerce, healthcare, and industrial products and services, principally located in the New Hampshire coastal region.
Investment: 250k - 2m
Business Type/Stage: Early Stage
Website: www.ecoastangels.com
Contact email: ecoastangels@gmail.com

Emergent Growth Fund
Location: Florida
Bio: Focusses on companies developing unique, leading-edge products, or proprietary technologies that possess the potential for rapid growth in significant markets.
Investment: 200 - 500k
Business Type/Stage: Early Stage
Website: www.emergentgrowth.com
Contact email: int@emergentgrowth.com

Enterprise Angels
Location: South Dakota
Bio: Their mission is to assist South Dakota's emerging growth entrepreneurs.
Business Type/Stage: Start up
Website: www.enterpriseangels.co.nz

eonCapital
Location: Colorado
Bio: eonCapital has assisted many entrepreneurs in launching, developing and growing various web-based businesses.
Investment: 5m
Business Type/Stage: Seed and Early Stage
Website: www.eoncapital.com
Contact email: inquiry@eoncapital.com
Contact tel: +1 3038509300

Floodgate
Location: Menlo Park
Currency: USD
Size: 270m
Bio: Mobile, curated web, enterprise software
Investment: 150k - 1m
Business Type/Stage: Start up
Website: www.floodgate.com
Contact email: businessplans@maples.net

Florida Angel Investors
Location: Florida
Bio: Florida Angel Investors aims to create networks and funds in the state of Florida.

Investment: 500k - 2m
Business Type/Stage: Early Stage
Website: www.floridaangel.com
Contact email: info2007@floridaangel.com

Founders Co-op
Location: Washington
Currency: USD
Size: 30m
Bio: Enterprise SaaS, marketplaces, finance, mobile
Business Type/Stage: Early Stage
Website: www.founderscoop.com
Contact email: chris@founderscoop.com

Fund for Arkansas' Future
Location: Arkansas
Currency: USD
Size: 6.5m
Bio: Angel investor fund launched in January, 2005 for the purpose of capitalizing Arkansas-based companies.
Business Type/Stage: Early Stage
Website: www.arkansasfund.com
Contact email: jeff@arkansasfund.com

FundingPost
Location: Newington, CT
Currency: USD
Size: 108bn
Bio: Investment network for entrepreneurs to find investors online.
Investment: 100 - 250k
Business Type/Stage: Early Stage
Website: www.fundingpost.com
Contact email: info@FundingPost.com

Gathering of Angels
Location: New Mexico
Bio: Capital for over 380 young entrepreneurial companies from 20K to 39M.
Business Type/Stage: Seed and Early Stage

Website: www.gatheringofangels.com
Contact email: admin@gatheringofangels.com

Golden Angels Network
Location: Wisconsin
Bio: Interested in high potential, high growth business investment opportunities.
Website: www.goldenangelsnetwork.org

Golden Seeds
Location: Connecticut
Currency: USD
Size: 26.5m
Bio: Games, e-commerce, biotechnology
Business Type/Stage: Early Stage
Website: www.goldenseeds.com
Contact email: info@goldenseeds.com

Grand Angels
Location: Michigan
Currency: USD
Size: 80m
Bio: Software, enterprise software, web hosting
Investment: 250k - 2m
Business Type/Stage: Early Stage
Website: www.grandangels.org
Contact email: info@grandangels.org

Granite State Angels (GSA)
Location: New Hampshire
Bio: Biotechnology, Health Care
Investment: 100k - 1m
Business Type/Stage: Early Stage
Website: www.granitestateangels.com
Contact email: wainwright@granitestateangels.com

Grape Arbor
Location: New York
Currency: USD

Size: 15m
Bio: Investments in advertising/marketing online, web 2.0/social networking, financial services (tech and non-tech), and software/web-enhanced services.
Business Type/Stage: Start up
Website: www.grapearborvc.com
Contact email: info@grapearborvc.com

Great Lakes Angels

Location: Michigan
Bio: Great Lakes Angels is committed to connecting local entrepreneurs with experienced, high net-worth individuals.
Investment: 50 - 250k
Business Type/Stage: Early Stage
Website: www.citysideventures.com

GSVlabs

Location: Redwood City
Bio: Focused on accelerating the high-growth, high-impact verticals of EdTech, sustainability, big data, and mobility.
Business Type/Stage: Start up
Website: www.gsvlabs.com
Contact email: info@gsvlabs.com

Gust

Location: New York
Currency: USD
Size: 1.8bn
Bio: Gust's SaaS funding platform provides all the tools entrepreneurs need to manage their funding process, from pitch to exit worldwide.
Investment: 150k - 3m
Business Type/Stage: Startup
Website: www.gust.com
Contact email: info@gust.com

Hampton Roads Angel Network

Location: Virginia
Bio: Hampton Roads Angel Network is a Hampton, Virginia-based angel investor group.

Business Type/Stage: Seed and Early Stage
Website: www.technologyhamptonroads.com
Contact email: danbell@hric.email

Hawaii Angels
Location: Hawaii
Currency: USD
Size: 30m
Bio: Investment network for equity investors
Business Type/Stage: Seed
Website: www.hawaiiangels.org

Heartland Angels
Location: Illinois
Business Type/Stage: Early Stage start-up
Website: www.heartlandangels.com
Contact email: info@heartlandangels.com

Hub Angels Investment Group
Location: Massachusetts
Currency: USD
Size: 5.5m
Bio: Matches active investors with technology-driven, start-up companies. Software, Finance, Analytics
Investment: 200k - 1m
Business Type/Stage: Early Stage
Website: www.hubangels.com
Contact email: info@hubangels.com

Hyde Park Angels
Location: Illinois
Bio: Provides a forum for entrepreneurial-minded members to invest in businesses, primarily located in the Midwest.
Business Type/Stage: Early Stage
Website: www.hydeparkangels.com

i2E
Location: Oklahoma
Currency: USD

Size: 11m
Bio: Software, heathcare, health and wellness, within Oklahoma.
Business Type/Stage: Early Stage
Website: www.i2e.org
Contact email: info@i2e.org

Innovation Works
Location: Pennsylvania
Currency: USD
Size: 24m
Bio: Software, biotechnology, curated web
Business Type/Stage: Early Stage
Website: www.innovationworks.org
Contact tel: +1 4126811520

Intelligent Systems
Location: Georgia
Currency: USD
Size: 25m
Bio: For those seeking solid value investments, Intelligent Systems is a long term player in the creation, growth and operation.
Business Type/Stage: Growth
Website: www.intelsys.com
Contact email: bherron@intelsys.com

Investors Circle
Location: Massachusetts
Currency: USD
Size: 200m
Bio: Digital media, advertising, women
Investment: 50k - 3m
Business Type/Stage: Seed and Early Stage
Website: www.investorscircle.net
Contact tel: +1 9192961166

IrishAngels
Location: Indiana
Bio: Internet and mobile, scientific and medical, social enterprise, software, and special markets.

Investment: 1 - 3m
Business Type/Stage: Early Stage
Website: www.irishangels.com

Jumpstart Angel Network
Location: New Jersey
Currency: USD
Size: 35m
Bio: Invests in technology companies in the Mid-Atlantic region.
Investment: 200k - 1m
Business Type/Stage: Early Stage
Website: www.jumpstartnj.com
Contact email: info@jumpstartnj.org
Contact tel: +1 8568131440

JumpStart Inc
Location: Ohio
Currency: USD
Size: 51m
Bio: Software, biotechnology, healthcare
Business Type/Stage: Early Stage
Website: www.jumpstartinc.org
Contact email: askjs@jumpstartInc.org

KAYWEB Angels
Location: New York
Bio: Provides development services and mentoring to web and mobile start-ups in exchange for equity.
Website: www.kaywebangels.com
Contact email: angels@kayweb.com

Kegonsa Partners
Location: Wisconsin
Currency: USD
Size: 10.7m
Bio: Social media, analytics, public transportation
Business Type/Stage: Seed
Website: www.kegonsapartners.com
Contact tel: +1 6082050100

Keiretsu Forum

Location: California/Washington
Currency: USD
Size: 16m
Bio: Biotechnology, software, games, life science, real estate, technology, consumer products, cleantech
Investment: 500k - 2m
Business Type/Stage: Early, Late, Debt
Website: www.keiretsuforum.com
Contact email: info@keiretsuforum.com

Kickstart

Location: Utah
Bio: Supports the best entrepreneurs in Utah and the Mountain West with capital, connections and intelligence to launch hyper-growth companies into the world.
Business Type/Stage: Seed
Website: www.kickstartseedfund.com
Contact email: hello@kickstartfund.com

Launchpad Venture Group

Location: Massachusetts
Bio: Biotechnology, finance, software
Investment: 100 - 500k
Business Type/Stage: Early Stage
Website: www.launchpadventuregroup.com

Life Science Angels (LSA)

Location: California
Currency: USD
Size: 50m
Bio: Biotechnology, healthcare, health and wellness
Investment: 2m
Business Type/Stage: Seed, Early and Late
Website: www.lifescienceangels.com
Contact tel: +1 4085411152

Long Island Angel Network

Location: New York

Bio: Focus on software and information technology, mobile apps, biotechnology, nanotechnology, medicine, energy, environmental technology.
Investment: 500k – 2m
Business Type/Stage: Early and Growth
Website: www.liangels.net

Main Street Ventures
Location: Massachusetts
Investment: 500k
Business Type/Stage: Growth
Website: www.mainstventures.org

Maine Angels
Location: Maine
Bio: Biotechnology, aquaculture, food beverage
Investment: 50 - 350k
Business Type/Stage: Early Stage
Website: www.maineangels.org
Contact email: contact@maineangels.org

Mid-America Angels (MAA)
Location: Kansas
Bio: Semiconductors, security, mobile security
Investment: 250k - 1.5m
Business Type/Stage: Early Stage
Website: www.midamericaangels.com
Contact email: rvaughn@ecjc.com

Mid-Atlantic Angel Group (MAG)
Location: Pennsylvania
Currency: USD
Size: 3.3m
Bio: Bridges the gap between angel funding and institutional venture capital funding. Serves the Greater Philadelphia region.
Website: www.magfund.com
Contact email: jsnellenburg@sep.benfranklin.org
justin@sep.benfranklin.org

Midwest Venture Alliance (MVA)

Location: Kansas
Bio: Accredited investors committed to investing in high-growth technology companies in Kansas and surrounding states.
Investment: 250k - 2m
Business Type/Stage: Seed and Early Stage
Website: www.midwestventure.com
Contact tel: +1 3166515900

Nashville Capital Network

Location: Tennessee
Bio: Identify, develop, and support promising high-growth companies.
Investment: 750k - 3m
Business Type/Stage: Start up and Early Stage
Website: www.nashvillecapital.com
Contact tel: +1 615454395

NCIC Capital Fund

Location: Ohio
Currency: USD
Size: 5m
Bio: Invest in growth-oriented, technology-based companies.
Investment: 200k - 1m
Business Type/Stage: Growth
Website: www.conservationfund.org
Contact email: ncif@conservationfund.org

Nebraska Angels

Location: Nebraska
Bio: Exchange information about investment opportunities in companies with ties to the state of Nebraska.
Business Type/Stage: Early Stage
Website: www.nebraskaangels.org
Contact email: info@nebraskaangels.org

NEW Capital Fund

Location: Wisconsin
Currency: USD
Size: 10m

Bio: Focus on investing in 10 to 12 companies located in and around the New North.
Business Type/Stage: Early Stage
Website: www.newcapitalfund.com
Contact email: bob.debruin@newcapitalfund.com

New Mexico Angels
Location: New Mexico
Currency: USD
Size: 10m
Bio: Their mission is to provide opportunities where members can obtain outstanding financial returns while accelerating companies to market leadership.
Business Type/Stage: Early Stage
Website: www.nmangels.com
Contact email: info@nmangels.com

New Vantage Group
Location: Washington
Bio: Manages venture funds for active angel investors.
Investment: 4m
Business Type/Stage: Early Stage
Website: www.newvantagegroup.com
Contact tel: +1 7032554930

New World Angels
Location: Florida
Bio: Private investors dedicated to providing equity capital to entrepreneurial companies based in South Florida.
Investment: 500k - 2.5m
Business Type/Stage: Early Stage
Website: www.newworldangels.com
Contact email: info@newworldangels.com

New York Angels
Location: New York
Currency: USD
Size: 100m
Bio: Members exchange information about investment opportunities in the North East and provide administrative support to help such companies grow to market leadership.

Investment: 100k – 1m
Business Type/Stage: Early Stage
Website: www.newyorkangels.com

North Coast Angel Fund
Location: Ohio
Currency: USD
Size: 14m
Bio: Focus on technology investments.
Investment: 250k
Business Type/Stage: Early Stage
Website: www.northcoastangelfund.com

North County Angels
Location: Vermont
Bio: Biotechnology, healthcare, video streaming
Business Type/Stage: Early Stage
Website: www.northcountryangels.com
Contact email: ldissinger@merritt-merritt.com

Northwest Angel Network
Location: Idaho
Contact tel: +1 2084248438

NYC Seed
Location: New York
Currency: USD
Size: 2m
Bio: Software, SaaS, mobile
Investment: 200k
Business Type/Stage: Early Stage
Website: www.nycseed.com
Contact email: apply@nycseed.com

Ohio TechAngel Fund
Location: Ohio
Bio: Life sciences, information technology and physical sciences. Ohio-based technology investment opportunities.

Investment: 150k - 1m
Business Type/Stage: Early Stage
Website: www.ohiotechangels.com

Oregon Angel Fund

Location: Oregon
Currency: USD
Size: 8m
Bio: All sectors. Focus on start-ups that can scale quickly.
Investment: 100k - 2.5m
Business Type/Stage: Start up, Early, Growth
Website: www.oregonangelfund.com
Contact email: lynn@oregonangelfund.com

Origin Investment Group

Location: Wisconsin
Bio: Invest in high-potential businesses that seek equity funding for growth and expansion.
Business Type/Stage: Growth
Website: www.origininvestments.com/team

Pasadena Angels

Location: California
Bio: Technology-based ventures located in Southern California.
Investment: 1m
Business Type/Stage: Early Stage
Website: www.pasadenaangels.com

PCN ArchAngels

Location: California
Bio: Collection of 47 Family Offices from the United States
Business Type/Stage: Later Stage
Website: www.archangelsinvestors.com
Contact: doug@archangelsinvestors.com

Phenomenelle Angels Fund

Location: Wisconsin
Bio: Invests in women and minority owned or managed businesses in Wisconsin

and the Midwest. Information technology, life sciences, communications and consumer goods and services.

Investment: 100 - 500k
Business Type/Stage: Early Stage
Website: www.phenomenelleangels.com
Contact email: info@phenomenelleangels.com

Piedmont Angel Network

Location: North Carolina
Bio: Software, social media, advertising
Investment: 500k - 2m
Business Type/Stage: Early Stage
Website: www.piedmontangelnetwork.com
Contact email: dgrein@piedmontangelnetwork.com

Pocono Mountains Angel Network

Location: Pennsylvania
Bio: Homeland security, advanced manufacturing, healthcare, information technology, life sciences/biotechnology, and financial services.
Business Type/Stage: Early Stage
Website: www.esu.edu
Contact email: mgildea1@esu.edu

Portland Angel Network

Location: Oregon
Investment: 500k - 2m
Business Type/Stage: Early Stage

Private Capital Network

Location: California
Bio: Investment in the Southern California region
Business Type/Stage: Early Stage
Website: www.privatecapitalnetwork.net
Contact email: doug@privatecapitalnetwork.net

Private Investors Forum

Location: Pennsylvania
Bio: Providing private investors with private equity deals in SMEs and entrepreneurs.

Investment: 3 - 5m
Business Type/Stage: Early Stage
Website: www.private-investors.co.uk

Propel(x)
Location: San Francisco
Bio: Invest in deep technology start-ups - companies rooted in a ground-breaking scientific discovery or technological innovation.
Investment: 5 - 25k
Business Type/Stage: Seed, Series A & B
Website: www.propelx.com

Puget Sound Venture Club
Location: Washington
Currency: USD
Size: 92m
Bio: Cleantech, software
Business Type/Stage: Early Stage
Website: www.pugetsoundvc.com
Contact email: grritner@msn.com

Queen City Angels
Location: South Carolina
Currency: USD
Size: 45m
Bio: IT, bioscience, advanced materials, among others
Investment: 10k - 1m
Business Type/Stage: Early Stage
Website: www.qca.com

RAIN Source Capital
Location: Minnesota
Currency: USD
Size: 20m
Bio: Provides each RAIN fund with legal templates, investment tools, management expertise, and financing experience.
Business Type/Stage: Early Stage
Website: www.rainsourcecapital.com
Contact tel: +1 6516322140

River Valley Investors

Location: Massachusetts
Bio: Source of capital for start-ups in Western Massachusetts.
Investment: 100k - 1m
Business Type/Stage: Early Stage
Website: www.rivervalleyinvestors.com

Robin Hood Ventures

Location: Pennsylvania
Bio: Biotechnology, software, IT, life sciences
Investment: 250 - 500k
Business Type/Stage: Early Stage
Website: www.robinhoodventures.com
Contact email: info@robinhoodventures.com

Rochester Angel Network

Location: New York
Currency: USD
Size: 2.3m
Bio: Hardware + Software, sustainability, manufacturing
Investment: 250k - 2m
Business Type/Stage: Early Stage
Website: www.rochesterangels.com
Contact tel: +1 5852142400

Rockies Venture Club

Location: Colorado
Currency: USD
Size: 10m
Business Type/Stage: Early Stage
Website: www.rockiesventureclub.org
Contact email: info@rockiesventureclub.org

Sacramento Angels

Location: California
Bio: Software, curated web, enterprise software, life sciences, hardware
Business Type/Stage: Early Stage
Website: www.sacangels.com

Saint Louis Arch Angels

Location: Missouri
Bio: Accelerating companies to market leadership in the St Louis region.
Investment: 250k - 2m
Business Type/Stage: Early Stage
Website: www.stlouisarchangels.com

Salt Lake Life Science Angels

Location: Utah
Bio: Biotechnology, software, heathcare
Investment: 50 - 500k
Business Type/Stage: Early Stage
Website: www.sllsa.com

San Antonio Angels

Location: Texas
Bio: Development services, know-how, and advice benefit the business objectives of those technology-based opportunities seeking support.
Business Type/Stage: Early Stage

Sand Hill Angels

Location: California
Bio: Invests in internet, information technology, clean tech, consumer, and life sciences businesses.
Business Type/Stage: Seed, Early, Later Stage
Website: www.sandhillangels.com

SATAI

Location: Texas
Currency: USD
Size: 200m
Bio: SATAI's major focus is on growing new businesses.

Seed Capital Fund

Location: New York
Bio: Technology
Business Type/Stage: Early Stage
Website: www.scfcny.com
Contact email: nasir@scfcny.com

Seraph Capital Forum
Location: Washington
Bio: The first all women angel investor group created in the United States.
Business Type/Stage: Early Stage
Website: www.seraphcapital.com
Contact email: info@seraphcapital.com

Sierra Angels
Location: Nevada
Bio: Provides local technology ventures with funding, support, mentoring and connections. Sierra Angels has funded greater than 60 companies in a wide range of industries, including software, internet, wireless, social media, IT, healthtech, and cleantech.
Business Type/Stage: Seed Stage
Website: www.sierraangels.com

Silicom Ventures
Location: California
Bio: Central focus is on technology companies, with an emphasis on Wisconsin's core industries
Website: www.silicomventures.com
Contact email: contact@silicomventures.com

Silicon Pastures
Location: Wisconsin
Bio: Consider numerous technology and industry sectors, including traditional manufacturing, high-tech, and biotech.
Investment: 60k - 1.9m
Website: www.siliconpastures.com
Contact email: teresa@siliconpastures.com

Social Leverage
Location: Arizona
Bio: Invests in exceptional entrepreneurs in the technology space.
Investment: 100 - 500k
Business Type/Stage: All stages
Website: www.socialleverage.com

Space Angels Network
Location: Virginia
Bio: Focused on aerospace-related opportunities.
Business Type/Stage: Early Stage
Website: www.spaceangelsnetwork.com
Contact email: info@spaceangelsnetwork.com

Startup Florida
Location: Florida
Bio: Promotes the creation and acceleration of technology businesses by providing capital, mentoring and a supportive community for entrepreneurs.
Business Type/Stage: Early Stage
Website: www.startupflorida.com
Contact email: richswier@gmail.com

Startup Grind
Location: Palo Alto
Bio: World's largest community connecting entrepreneurs, founders, CEOs, innovators, educators and investors.

Startup Hive
Location: California
Bio: Assists emerging technology.
Business Type/Stage: Start up
Website: www.startuphive.wordpress.com
Contact email: info@startuphive.co

Stateline Angels
Location: Ilinois
Bio: Angel investor organization that provides investment capital.
Business Type/Stage: Early Stage
Website: www.statelineangels.com

Tech Coast Angels
Location: California
Currency: USD
Size: 48m
Bio: Software, curated web, biotechnology

Investment: 250k - 2m
Business Type/Stage: Seed, Early and Late
Website: www.techcoastangels.com

Tech Valley Angel Network

Location: New York
Bio: Invests in technology companies that are located within 150 miles of Albany, New York.
Investment: 1m
Business Type/Stage: Growth
Website: www.techvalleyangels.com
Contact email: peterp@ceg.org

Technology Tree Group

Location: Texas
Bio: Technology investment opportunities for private research organizations and companies bringing new technologies to market.
Business Type/Stage: Early Stage

TechRanch

Location: Montana
Bio: TechRanch works with Montana-based high tech entrepreneurs to help them launch and build profitable, long-term operating companies in Montana.
Business Type/Stage: Early Stage
Website: www.techranchaustin.com
Contact email: info@techranchaustin.com

TechStars

Location: Colorado
Bio: Techstars is a start-up accelerator that provides mentorship-driven investment services for technology-oriented companies.
Investment: 18k
Website: www.techstars.com
Contact tel: +1 3037206559

Tevel Angel Club

Location: New York
Bio: Invests in Israeli technology companies.

Website: www.tevelglobal.com
Contact email: info@tevelglobal.com

Texas Women Ventures Fund
Location: Texas
Bio: Help women-owned businesses reach their full potential.
Investment: 750k
Website: www.texaswomenventures.com
Contact email: info@texaswomenventures.com

Tgap Ventures
Location: Michigan
Bio: Healthcare, advertising, hardware
Investment: 500k - 1m
Website: www.tgapventures.com
Contact email: pete@farner.net

The Angels Forum
Location: California
Bio: Biotechnology, video streaming, video
Website: www.angelsforum.com
Contact tel: +1 6508570700

The Atlantis Group
Location: North Carolina
Contact tel: +1 9198064340

Theorem Ventures
Location: San Francisco
Bio: Technology related companies
Business Type/Stage: Seed
Website: www.theoremventures.com
Contact email: hello@theoremventures.com

Tri-State Private Investor Network
Location: New York
Business Type/Stage: Early Stage
Website: www.angelinvestorfunding.com
Contact email: ellen@angelinvestorfunding.com

MedPro Investors LLCs
Location: New York
Bio: Biotechnology, healthcare, medical devices .
Investment: 250k - 2m
Business Type/Stage: Early Stage
Website: www.medproinvestors.com
Contact email: Steve@MedProInvestors.com
                  Isaac@MedProInvestors.com

Tugboat Ventures
Location: California
Bio: E-commerce, advertising, SaaS
Website: www.tugboatventures.com
Contact email: share@thetugboatgroup.com

Twin Cities Angels
Location: Minnesota
Investment: 25k - 2m
Business Type/Stage: Seed and Early Stage
Website: www.twincitiesangels.com

Utah Angels
Location: Utah
Currency: USD
Size: 16m
Bio: The Utah Angels are a group of fifteen private investors backing Utah entrepreneurs.
Website: www.ua2.co

Venture Investment Forum (Ben Franklin)
Location: Pennsylvania
Bio: Funding and business support services to tech-based start-ups and small manufacturers located in our 32-county footprint.
Investment: 500k
Business Type/Stage: Growth
Website: www.cnp.benfranklin.org
Contact email: info@cnp.benfranklin.org

Virginia Active Angels Network

Location: Virginia
Bio: VAAN team combines energy, expertise and entrepreneurs to encourage networking opportunities with angel investors throughout Virginia.
Website: www.virginiaactiveangelnetwork.com

Walnut Venture Associates

Location: Massachusetts
Bio: Entrepreneurs and investors seeking investment opportunities in companies in the New England area. Focused on information technology.
Investment: 250K - 1m
Business Type/Stage: Seed & Early Stage
Website: www.walnutventures.com
Contact email: info@walnutventures.com

Wider Wake

Location: New York
Bio: Global business consultancy that specializes in advising companies and entrepreneurs within the digital media and content ecosystem.
Business Type/Stage: Seed
Website: www.widerwake.net
Contact email: enquiries@widerwake.net

Willow Garage

Location: California
Bio: Focused on developing the next generation of robotic devices.
Website: www.willowgarage.com
Contact email: info@willowgarage.com

Wilmington Investor Network

Location: North Carolina
Bio: Provides capital to companies in Eastern, North and South Carolina. Focus on technology, biotechnology, and medical device companies, but will consider other business ventures with high-return potential.
Investment: 200 - 500k
Business Type/Stage: Early Stage
Website: www.wilmingtoninvestor.com
Contact email: info@wilmingtoninvestor.com

Wisconsin Investment Partners

Location: Wisconsin
Currency: USD
Size: 22m
Bio: Life science and technology
Investment: 300k
Business Type/Stage: Early Stage
Website: www.wisinvpartners.com
Contact email: tyaktus@wisinvpartners.com

Women's Investment Network

Location: Pennsylvania
Bio: Greater Philadelphia region's only organization specifically for women who are leaders of and investors in high-growth businesses.
Investment: 250k - 2m
Business Type/Stage: Early Stage
Website: www.thewomensinvestmentnetwork.com

X/Seed Capital

Location: California
Business Type/Stage: Seed
Website: www.xseedcap.com
Contact email: info@xseedcap.com

Zino Society

Location: Washington
Bio: Angel investors, entrepreneurs and connectors that propel businesses and investors to success through active angel investing, consulting and mentoring.
Investment: 25 - 100k
Business Type/Stage: Early Stage
Website: www.zinosociety.com
Contact tel: +1 2065296500

Zygote Ventures

Location: California
Bio: Invest in innovative technology enterprises.
Investment: 1m
Business Type/Stage: Early Stage
Website: www.argentum.no
Contact email: info@zygoteventures.com

2.6

REST OF WORLD CAPITAL INVESTORS

Alliance Entreprendre
Location: Paris
Currency: EUR
Size: 64m
Investment: 200m
Portfolio: Geotec, Paragraph +
Website: www.allianceentreprendre.com
Contact email: contact@allianceentreprendre.com

21 Partners
Location: Treviso, Milan
Currency: USD
Size: 319m
Targeting: Italy, France, Poland
Bio: Bringing vision, growth and efficieny to the mid market. Targets SMEs.
Portfolio: Poligof, Impact, Adesso +
Website: www.21investimenti.it
Contact email: info@21investimenti.it
Contact tel: +39 277121311

360 Capital Partners

Location: Luxembourg, Germany
Currency: USD
Size: 135m
Targeting: France, Italy
Bio: Address the growth of tech start-ups in Europe.
Investment: 300k - 1m
Portfolio: Adomos, finance, Arkena
Stage: Early & Mid Stage
Website: www.360capitalpartners.com
Contact email: info@360capitalpartners.com
Contact tel: +352 621294505

3TS Venture Partners

Location: Vienna
Currency: USD
Size: 266m
Targeting: Central and Eastern Europe
Bio: Technology focused private equity and venture capital firms. technology & internet, media & communications and technology-enabled services.
Investment: 300k - 10m
Portfolio: EIF, EBRD, Cisco, OTP, Sitra, 3i and KfW +
Stage: Early & Mid Stage
Website: www.3tscapital.com
Contact email: info@3tscapital.com
Contact tel: +43 18901698

4th Level Ventures

Location: Dublin, Ireland
Currency: EUR
Size: 20m
Targeting: Ireland
Bio: They are focused exclusively on investing in companies whose Intellectual Property arises from third level education institutional research. Their primary objective is to commercialise the business opportunities that arise from university research.
Portfolio: Celtic Catalysts, Powervation Limited +
Stage: Early & Mid Stage

Website: www.4thlevelventures.ie
Contact email: info@4thlevelventures.ie
Contact tel: +353 16333627

AAC Capital Partners
Location: Amsterdam, Stockholm, London
Currency: EUR
Size: 1.66bn
Targeting: Worldwide
Bio: Growth orientated investor. Buyouts – companies have clear growth path underpinned by a macro trend. Leading market position – local/global, multiple and tangible value drivers. Strong management that co-invests. Investments – Industrial, Consumer and Business Services.
Investment: 50 - 500m
Portfolio: Viking
Stage: Buy Out
Website: www.aaccapitalpartners.com
Contact email: info@aaccapitalpartners.com
Contact tel: +31 203331308

Accel Partners
Location: Palo Alto, Silicon Valley, New York, Bangalore, London
Currency: USD
Size: 17bn
Targeting: Worldwide
Bio: Invest into what they call 'category-defining technology companies'. Consumer internet, digital media, mobile.
Investment: 500k - 50m
Portfolio: Spotify, Lynda, Etsy +
Stage: Late Stage
Website: www.accel.com
Contact tel: +44 2071701000

ACT Venture Capital
Location: Dublin, Ireland
Currency: USD
Size: 29m
Targeting: Europe and USA

Bio: Investment interest in technology, mobile, internet, healthcare and financial market opportunities.
Investment: 200k - 30m
Portfolio: CR2, CapeClear, Novate +
Stage: Early & Mid Stage
Website: www.actventure.com
Contact email: info@actvc.ie
Contact tel: +353 12600966

Acton Capital Partners
Location: Munich, Germany
Currency: USD
Size: 470m
Targeting: Europe and North America
Bio: Specialist investor in internet and mobile-based, consumer-oriented businesses.
Portfolio: Mytheresa, Etsy, Zooplus, AbeBooks, HolidayCheck and Onvista +
Stage: Early, Mid and Late
Website: www.actoncapital.com
Contact email: info@actoncapital.de
Contact tel: +49 8924218870

Adara Venture Partners
Location: Luxemburg
Currency: USD
Size: 120m
Targeting: Worldwide
Bio: Technology based ventures
Portfolio: Alien Vault, Stratio +
Website: www.adaravp.com
Contact email: info@adaravp.com
Contact tel: +352 4818283940

Alegro Advisors
Location: Germany
Targeting: Europe, USA, Asia
Bio: Independent corporate finance advisory firm focusing on clients across Europe.

Website: www.alegrocapital.com
Contact email: info@alegroadvisors.com

Ambient Sound Investments
Location: Talinn
Currency: EUR
Size: 100m
Targeting: Asia, Europe, USA
Bio: Games, software, hardware
Investment: 500k
Portfolio: Clifton, DailyPerfect, Ecofleet +
Stage: Early Stage
Website: www.asi.ee
Contact email: info@asi.ee

Ayondo (Previously - Next Generation Finance Invest)
Location: Switzerland
Currency: USD
Size: 28m
Targeting: Europe
Bio: Fintech based
Portfolio: Gekko, OANDA, Ayondo and StockPulse +
Website: www.ayondo.com
Contact email: support@ayondo.com
Contact tel: +440 2033300865

Azione Capital
Location: Singapore
Targeting: Asia
Bio: Focused approach to mentoring, incubating and investing in interactive digital media, mobile communications, energy and maritime industry start-ups that operate primarily within Asia.
Stage: Seed
Website: www.azionecapital.com
Contact email: startup@azionecapital.com
Contact tel: +65 31121688

Backstage

Location: Gothenburg, Sweden
Bio: VC firm primarily investing in unlisted Scandinavian entrepreneurial companies.
Stage: Early
Website: www.backstage.se
Contact tel: +46 31815710

BaltCap

Location: Estonia, Latvia and Lithuania
Currency: USD
Size: 84m
Targeting: Baltic based
Bio: Ticketing, Start-ups, Mobile Commerce.
Investment: 3 - 3m
Stage: Start-ups
Website: www.baltcap.com
Contact email: info@baltcap.com

BASF Venture Capital

Location: Ludwigshafen, Germany
Targeting: Worldwide
Bio: Chemicals, plastics, performance products, functional solutions, agricultural solutions, oil and gas, technology funds
Investment: 1 - 5m
Portfolio: Arcadia, SmartKem +
Stage: Start-ups/other VCs
Website: www.basf-vc.de
Contact tel: +49 6216076801

BBVA Ventures

Location: Madrid, San Francisco
Currency: USD
Size: 100m
Targeting: USA, EU
Bio: BBVA Ventures provides funding and expertise to promising technology companies disrupting financial services.

Portfolio: Prosper, DocuSign, Simple, Radius, Coinbase, SumUp, Personal Capital and Ribbit Capital +
Stage: Early, Mid & Late Stage
Website: www.bbvaventures.com

BDMI
Location: Berlin, New York
Currency: EUR
Size: 16bn
Targeting: North America, Europe, Israel
Bio: Digital Media
Investment: 0.5 - 4m
Portfolio: Seedcamp, Dealvertise +
Stage: Early Stage
Website: www.bdmifund.com
Contact email: info@bdmifund.com
Contact tel: +49 30747844096

Bonnier Growth Media
Location: Stockholm
Currency: SEK
Size: 2bn
Bio: Digital Media, Marketplaces, Mobile, Content platforms, Software
Stage: Seed, Early and Later
Website: www.bonniergrowthmedia.com
Contact email: bgm@bonnier.se

Capricorn Venture Partners
Location: Leuven, Belgium
Currency: USD
Size: 55m
Targeting: Europe
Bio: Invests in innovative companies with technology as competitive advantage: ICT, healthtech, cleantech.
Investment: 0.5 - 5m
Stage: Early and Late
Website: www.capricorn.be
Contact email: capricorn@capricorn.be

Chalmers Innovation
Location: Gothenburg, Sweden
Bio: Software, health, wellness
Investment: 15m
Portfolio: 1928 Diagnostics, Acosense +
Stage: Seed and Start-ups
Website: www.chalmersventures.com
Contact email: info@chalmersventures.com

Cipio Partners
Location: Luxembourg
Currency: EUR
Size: 300m
Targeting: Europe
Bio: Software, semiconductors, communications, internet/media and other technologies
Investment: 3 - 30m
Portfolio: B2X, Openet, Falcon.IO, EyeEm, Brightpearl
Stage: Secondary direct and growth
Website: www.cipiopartners.com
Contact email: info@cipiopartners.com
Contact tel: +352 (26) 20 10 54

Cleantech Invest
Location: Helsinki
Currency: EUR
Size: 180m
Investment: 1 - 2m
Portfolio: Nuuka, Nocart +
Website: www.cleantechinvest.com
Contact email: bigge@cleantechinvest.com

Connect Ventures
Location: London
Currency: USD
Size: 33m
Targeting: Europe
Bio: Internet and mobile

Investment: 200k - 1m
Stage: Early Stage and Start-ups
Website: www.connectventures.co.uk

Delta Partners
Location: Dublin
Currency: USD
Size: 246m
Targeting: UK, Ireland
Bio: Targets early stage technology and MedTech companies.
Portfolio: Betapond, BlikBook, Fishtree
Stage: Late Stage
Website: www.deltapartners.com
Contact email: info@deltapartners.com
Contact tel: +44 2036429329

E.Ventures
Location: San Francisco, Berlin
Currency: USD
Size: 130m
Targeting: Worldwide
Bio: Global venture capital firm backing internet and software founders.
Investment: 100k - 10m
Portfolio: CityDeal, KaufDa, Farfetch.com +
Stage: Early Stage
Website: www.eventures.vc
Contact email: info@eventures.vc
Contact tel: +1 4158695200

Earlybird Venture Capital
Location: Berlin, Munich, Istanbul
Currency: USD
Size: 200m
Targeting: Worldwide
Bio: Invests across multiple stages. Their companies have the potential to reshape markets and change the world around us.
Investment: 250k - 10m
Portfolio: Wunderlist, EyeEm +

Stage: Early & Mid Stage
Website: www.earlybird.com
Contact tel: +49 3046724700

Excel Partners
Location: Madrid
Targeting: Latin America, Portugal, Spain
Bio: Specialize in investments in biotechnology in medium-sized companies.
Investment: 2.5 - 62m
Website: www.excel-partners.com
Contact email: admin@excel-partners.com
Contact tel: +34 2039786200

Faber Ventures
Location: Portugal
Bio: Invest in new internet companies.
Portfolio: Advicefront, Chicbychoice, Gitter +
Stage: Pre, Seed and Post-Seed
Website: www.faber-ventures.com
Contact email: contact@faber-ventures.com

FinLeap
Location: Berlin
Bio: Provides funding for bold ideas, supporting entrepreneurs who are building scalable businesses and solving real problems in the financial industry.
Investment: 0.5 - 5m
Portfolio: Savedo, BillFront, Clarks +
Stage: Early Stage
Website: www.finleap.com
Contact email: berlin@finleap.com

General Atlantic
Location: New York, London, Munich, Amsterdam
Targeting: Worldwide
Portfolio: Adyen, Avant and Klarna +
Website: www.generalatlantic.com
Contact tel: +44 2074843200

Gilde Healthcare Partners
Location: Boston, Netherlands
Currency: USD
Size: 200m
Targeting: Europe, USA
Bio: Investor in fast growing healthcare technology and healthcare services companies.
Investment: 20m
Stage: Multiple
Website: www.gildehealthcare.com
Contact email: healthcare@gildehealthcare.com
Contact tel: +31 302192565

Hasso Plattner Ventures
Location: Potsdam
Targeting: Europe, South Africa, USA
Bio: Invests in fast-growing, information technology-driven companies.
Investment: 250k - 10m
Portfolio: Delivery Hero, HitFox, SponsorPay +
Stage: Seed
Website: www.hp-ventures.com
Contact tel: +49 33197992101

HealthCap
Location: Sweden
Currency: EUR
Size: 1bn
Targeting: Europe, UK, USA
Bio: Biotechnology, healthcare, messaging
Portfolio: 102+
Stage: Early, Mid & Late Stage
Website: www.healthcap.eu
Contact tel: +46 84425850

Highland Capital Partners Europe
Location: Geneva, Boston, Palo Alto and Shanghai
Currency: USD
Size: 379m
Targeting: European, Global ambition

Bio: Invest in rapidly growing European internet, mobile and software companies that address large market opportunities.
Investment: 10 - 30m
Portfolio: Adjust, eGYM, ShopFully +
Website: www.highlandeurope.com
Contact tel: +41 228177200

Holtzbrinck Ventures

Location: Germany
Currency: USD
Size: 331m
Targeting: Europe
Bio: Consumer internet and enablers
Investment: 0.5 - 40m
Portfolio: Zalando, Groupon, Delivery Hero +
Stage: Early & Mid Stage
Website: www.holtzbrinck-ventures.com
Contact email: information@holtzbrinck.net

i5invest

Location: Vienna
Targeting: Europe, USA
Bio: Grows the successful web and mobile business models of tomorrow. They focus specifically on B2C Web 2.0 ventures.
Stage: Seed
Website: www.i5invest.com
Contact email: vienna@i5invest.com

Jerusalem Venture Partners

Location: Jerusalem
Currency: USD
Size: 1bn
Targeting: Israel, UK, USA, Asia
Bio: Cyber Security, Big Data, Mobile, Media, Software, Enterprise Software, IOT, Storage
Investment: 1 - 50m
Portfolio: CyberArk Software, QlikTech, CyActive
Stage: Seed, Early & Late

Website: www.jvpvc.com
Contact email: info@bakehila.org.il
Contact tel: +972 29669995

Kima Ventures
Location: Paris, London
Targeting: Worldwide
Bio: Companies in internet industry
Investment: 100 - 200 k
Portfolio: Camera51, Lyft, and Open Garden +
Stage: Seed to series A
Website: www.kimaventures.com

Life.SREDA
Location: Moscow, Singapore
Currency: USD
Size: 100m
Targeting: USA, Western and Eastern Europe
Bio: Focus on investments in the fintech, mobile and internet sectors.
Portfolio: Rocketbank, SumUp, Anthemis Group, Settle, Fidor Bank, Simple and Moven +
Stage: Seed & Early Stage
Website: www.lifesreda.com
Contact email: info@lifesreda.ru

Mangrove Capital Partners
Location: Luxembourg
Currency: USD
Size: 365m
Targeting: Greater Europe
Bio: Focus on internet and software companies
Investment: 15 - 20m
Portfolio: Skype, Wix, brands4friends, Nimbuzz +
Stage: Early & Mid Stage
Website: www.mangrove.vc
Contact email: deals@mangrove.vc
Contact tel: +352 2625341

Nexit Ventures

Location: Helsinki
Currency: USD
Size: 95m
Targeting: Nordic region, USA
Bio: Mobile, software, games
Website: www.nexitventures.com
Contact tel: +358 96818910

Northzone Ventures

Location: Stockholm, Oslo, Copenhagen, London
Currency: USD
Size: 757m
Targeting: Europe
Bio: Invest in the technology industry. Focus mainly on advertising, software and curated web.
Portfolio: Seed, Early Stage, Late-Stage, and Private Equity Investments.
Stage: Sticky, Fishbrain, Test Freaks +
Website: www.northzone.com
Contact email: info@northzone.com

Partech Ventures

Location: Paris, Berlin, San Francisco
Currency: USD
Size: 240m
Targeting: Worldwide
Bio: Technology companies and digital media
Investment: 200k - 50m
Portfolio: Made.com, Qype, Daily Motion +
Stage: Early & Mid Stage
Website: www.partechventures.com
Contact email: sjameau@partechventures.com

Point Nine

Location: Berlin
Currency: USD
Size: 113m
Targeting: Worldwide
Bio: SaaS, e-commerce, mobile, marketplaces

Investment: 100k - 1m
Portfolio: Couchsurfing, Dawanda +
Stage: Early Stage
Website: www.pointninecap.com
Contact email: info@pointninecap.com

Principia
Location: Milan, Italy
Currency: EUR
Size: 80m
Targeting: Italy
Bio: 3 funds: I - Dedicated to investments in innovative businesses born thanks to academic or industrial research. II - The fund's investments are focused on process innovation or product through digital technologies. III - Specifically dedicated to the healthcare sector.
Portfolio: Focuses on small & medium sized enterprises
Stage: Early & Mid Stage
Website: www.principiasgr.it
Contact email: info@principiasgr.it

Rhodium
Location: Israel
Targeting: Israel, New York, Silicon Valley
Bio: Works closely with passionate founders, first-timers as well as serial entrepreneurs, in the fields of advertising, social, mobile, e-commerce and other exceptional technologies.
Portfolio: Yotpo and Rounds +
Stage: Early Stage
Website: www.rhodium.co.il
Contact tel: +972 99606900

Robert Bosch Venture Capital
Location: Germany, Stuttgart
Targeting: Worldwide
Bio: Tech Companies. First and Second Round
Investment: 1 - 10m
Portfolio: Alpine, Flybits, Flyby
Stage: Early and Late

Website: www.rbvc.com
Contact tel: +49 71181147961

Rockaway Capital
Location: Prague, Sao Paulo, San Francisco
Currency: USD
Size: 253m
Targeting: Worldwide
Bio: Builds the Internet economy in emerging markets. Looking for technology start-ups.
Portfolio: SPORTY, SnowBoards, BigBrands +
Stage: Early & Mid Stage
Website: www.rockawaycapital.com
Contact email: info@rockawaycapital.com

SEED Capital
Location: Copenhagen, Denmark
Currency: USD
Size: 224m
Targeting: Denmark, Southern Sweden
Bio: Invests in high-growth tech startups
Investment: 250 - 750k
Portfolio: Trustpilot, Vivino, Templafy
Stage: Early & Mid Stage
Website: www.seedcapital.dk
Contact email: info@seedcapital.dk

Seventure Partners
Location: Paris
Currency: EUR
Size: 500m
Targeting: Europe
Bio: Information and Communication Technologies (ICT) and Life Sciences (LF).
Investment: 0.5 - 0.9m
Stage: Early & Late Stage
Website: www.seventure.fr
Contact email: contact-lifesciences@seventure.ch

Shenzhen Capital Group
Location: China
Currency: JPY
Size: 2.5bn
Bio: Provide venture capital-related value-added services that promote the development of high-tech industries in China.
Portfolio: Bocom, Senodia +
Stage: Early & Late Stage
Website: www.szvc.com.cn
Contact email: master@szvc.com.cn

Singulariteam
Location: Israel
Currency: USD
Bio: Focuses on the development of technology based companies, by providing capital and additional supporting services. Focuses on the fields of artificial intelligence, robotics, augmented reality, virtual reality and other industry-leading technologies in various fields.
Portfolio: Soluto, AngelList, and BillGuard +
Website: www.singulariteam.com
Contact email: info@singulariteam.com

Sunstone Capital
Location: Copenhagen
Currency: USD
Size: 111m
Targeting: Northern and Eastern Europe
Bio: Invests in software, mobile and and internet companies with global potential.
Investment: 200k - 2m
Portfolio: Issuu, Gidsy, Amen +
Website: www.sunstone.eu
Contact email: info@sunstone.eu

TA Associates
Location: London, Boston, Menlo Park, Mumbai and Hong Kong
Currency: USD
Size: 4bn
Targeting: North America, Europe, India, Asia

Bio: Invests in growing private companies in exciting industries including fintech, technology, financial services, healthcare and consumer businesses and communications.
Investment: 50 - 500m
Portfolio: Bats, Creditex +
Stage: Private Equity
Website: www.ta.com
Contact tel: +44 2078230200

Technology Crossover Ventures (TCV)
Location: Palo Alto, Silicon Valley, New York, London
Currency: USD
Size: 9.9bn
Targeting: North America, Europe
Bio: Provides financial, strategic and operational support for today's rapidly growing, innovative tech companies.
Investment: 10 - 100m
Portfolio: Merkle, WorldRemit, Elevate, Think Finance and Trading Screen +
Stage: Early, Late and Private Equity
Website: www.tcv.com
Contact email: ir@tcv.com

Tengelmann Ventures
Location: Mülheim an der Ruhr
Targeting: Worldwide
Bio: Focus on early and later stage investment in consumer internet companies, internet marketplaces and technology ventures.
Portfolio: Mülheim an der Ruhr +
Stage: Early & Late Stage
Website: www.tev.de
Contact email: ideas@e-tengelmann.de

T-Ventures - Deutsche Telekom Capital Partners
Location: Germany
Currency: USD
Size: 620m
Targeting: Europe

Bio: Focus on Germany's exciting and growing tech start-up scene. Economic and technological synergies with Deutsche Telekom's business units.
Investment: 500k - 5m
Portfolio: 6wunderkinder, Moviepilot, MyTaxi +
Stage: Early, Mid & Late Stage
Website: www.telekom.com

Venista Ventures

Location: Germany
Targeting: Europe, USA
Bio: Specializes in smart mobile ideas based on profound market experience. Mobile, internet, venture capital, wireless, apps.
Investment: 50 - 300k
Portfolio: Startupbootcamp, Klash +
Stage: Early Stage
Website: www.venista-ventures.com
Contact email: info@venista.com

Venture Capital for Africa (VC4A)

Location: Amsterdam, Stockholm, London
Investment: 10k - 1m
Website: www.vc4africa.biz

Verve Capital Partners - investiere

Location: Zurich
Targeting: Europe
Bio: Aims to develop and implement innovative financing concepts for small and medium sized enterprises (SMEs) while connecting private investors directly to SME investments. Since February 2010 Verve Capital Partners operates investiere. ch: a new, agile form of financing, combining best practices of traditional venture capital with e-finance and social media.
Investment: 500k - 2.5m
Portfolio: Gmelin, TherabOptics, Arcbazar +
Stage: Early Stage
Website: www.investiere.ch
Contact email: www.investiere.ch

Viola Ventures

Location: Herzliya, Israel
Currency: USD
Size: 800m
Targeting: Israel or Israeli related
Bio: Invests across a number of key market segments including: software, new enterprise infrastructure, big data, digital media, consumer applications and semiconductors.
Investment: 1 - 10m
Portfolio: Kontera, Optimal, ECI +
Stage: Early Stage
Website: www.viola-group.com
Contact email: info@carmelventures.com
Contact tel: +972 99720400

2.7

REST OF WORLD
ANGEL NETWORKS

AfterDox
Location: Israel
Bio: Advertising, Curated Web, Writers
Investment: 100 - 500k
Business Type/Stage: Early Stage
Website: www.afterdox.com
Contact email: info@afterdox.com
Contact tel: +972 545511688

Akola Capital
Location: Barcelona
Bio: Mentorship and investments to start-ups
Contact email: guerrero@mababogados.com

Alfvén & Didrikson
Location: Stockholm
Bio: Seek investment opportunities in Northern Europe among small and mid sized privately held companies.
Business Type/Stage: Early Stage
Website: www.alfvendidrikson.com

Almi Invest
Location: Stockholm
Currency: SEK
Size: 1bn
Bio: Invests in Swedish companies with exciting, scalable business models and motivated entrepreneurs.
Investment: 25k - 1m
Business Type/Stage: Seed
Website: www.almi.se
Contact tel: +468 771558500

Angel Association New Zealand
Location: Auckland, New Zealand
Bio: Aim to increase the quantity, quality and success of angel investments in New Zealand and in doing so create a greater pool of capital for innovative companies.
Business Type/Stage: Start up
Website: www.angelassociation.co.nz
Contact tel: +1 649 3025218

Angel Forum
Location: Vancouver
Bio: Technology and non technology pre-screened companies
Investment: 100k - 1m
Website: www.angelforum.org
Contact email: chaworth@direct.ca

AngelVest
Location: Shanghai
Bio: Provides capital to companies with significant pre-existing and/or planned operations in China.
Investment: 100 - 500k
Business Type/Stage: Early Stage
Website: www.angelvestgroup.com
Contact email: contact@aamash.com

Angie.co
Location: Moscow
Website: www.kown.com
Contact email: team@angie.co

Argentum

Location: Bergen, Norway
Currency: NOK
Size: 10bn
Bio: Investments in Northern Europe and energy-focused private equity funds.
Website: www.argentum.no
Contact tel: +1 47 55547000

Australian Association of Angel Investors

Location: Australia
Bio: Investments in high-growth companies through professional and ethical conduct.
Business Type/Stage: Early Stage
Website: www.aaai.net.au
Contact email: info@email.com

Business Angel Institute

Location: Vienna, Austria
Bio: Goals to increase the number of active business angels in start-up ecosystems.
Website: www.businessangelinstitute.org
Contact tel: +431 930873036

Business Angels Agentur Ruhr e.V. (BAAR)

Location: Essen, Germany
Business Type/Stage: Start up
Website: www.baar-ev.de
Contact email: info@baar-ev.de
Contact tel: +49 01 8941530

Business Angels Copenhagen

Location: Denmark
Bio: BA-Copenhagen is interested in funding high-tech companies
Business Type/Stage: Start-up
Website: www.bacopenhagen.dk
Contact email: fps@keystones.dk

Business Angels Europe

Location: Brussels
Bio: Business Angels Europe is the voice of angel investing in Europe
Website: www.businessangelseurope.com
Contact email: info@businessangelseurope.com

Business Angels Netzwerk Deutschland e.V. (BAND)

Location: Germany
Bio: Umbrella organization of the German informal venture capital market.
Investment: 10 - 250k
Business Type/Stage: Start-up
Website: www.business-angels.de
Contact email: info@bostonseed.com

Butterfly Ventures

Location: Oulu, Finland
Currency: EUR
Size: 10m
Bio: Regional Companies
Investment: 200 – 400k
Business Type/Stage: Start-up
Website: www.butterfly.vc
Contact email: matti@butterfly.vc

Custodi di Successo

Location: Vicenza, Italy
Bio: Mechanics, ICT, health and biotechnology
Investment: 5 - 200k
Business Type/Stage: Early Stage
Website: www.custodidisuccesso.it

EstBAN

Location: Estonia
Bio: EstBAN is a circle of business angels based in Estonia.
Investment: 20 - 500k
Business Type/Stage: Start up
Website: www.estban.ee
Contact tel: +372 56249959

European Trade Association for Business Angels
Location: Brussels
Currency: EUR
Size: 7.5bn
Bio: Invests in Europe's SMEs
Investment: 25 - 500k
Business Type/Stage: Early Stage
Website: www.eban.org
Contact email: info@eban.org

EuroQuity
Location: Europe, Africa
Currency: EUR
Size: 300m
Bio: Puts growth companies in contact with development partners, particularly investors.
Investment: 500k - 3m
Business Type/Stage: Seed and Series A
Website: www.euroquity.com
Contact email: contact_en@euroquity.com

FIBAN Finnish Business Angels Network
Location: Helsinki & other cities, Finland
Bio: Quite tech-centric. Mainly European investment focus.
Investment: 100k
Business Type/Stage: Pre-seed & Seed
Website: www.fiban.org
Contact tel: +358 207350160

Food Angels
Location: Germany
Bio: German Food Angel Group
Business Type/Stage: Food Start-up
Website: www.food-angels.org
Contact email: info@food-angels.org

Fundme
Location: France
Bio: Funding from all sectors.
Business Type/Stage: Start-up and Early Stage
Website: www.fundme.fr
Contact email: clubs@fundme.co

Go Beyond
Location: Zurich
Bio: National, European, International
Investment: 150 - 500k
Business Type/Stage: Start-up
Website: www.go-beyond.biz
Contact tel: +41 445860098

Indian Angel Network
Location: New Delhi
Currency: USD
Size: 1m
Bio: Sectors considered: Sector agnostic as long as IAN has an investor with domain expertise.
Investment: 150k - 1m
Business Type/Stage: Startup and Early Stage

Invesdor OY
Location: Helsinki
Currency: EUR
Size: 10m
Bio: Fintech company that runs a pan-European debt and equity crowdfunding service.
Investment: 150k - 3m
Website: www.invesdor.com
Contact email: info@invesdor.com
Contact tel: +358 207352590

Italian Angels for Growth
Location: Italy
Bio: Supports entrepreneurship, innovation and research in Italy by helping to promote sustainable development in the long term.

Investment: 2m
Business Type/Stage: Early Stage
Website: www.italianangels.net
Contact email: press@italianangels.net
Contact tel: +39 276022952

Italian Business Angel Network
Location: Italy
Bio: Focused on the development and the growth of Business Angels phenomena in Italy.
Website: www.iban.it
Contact email: info@iban.it
Contact tel: +39 230516049

National Business Angels Association
Location: Moscow
Website: www.rvca.ru
Contact email: info@rusangels.ru

Paris Business Angels
Location: Paris, FR
Currency: EUR
Size: 4m
Bio: Invests in digital media and technology companies.
Investment: 200k - 1m
Business Type/Stage: Seed
Website: www.parisbusinessangels.com
Contact email: contact@parisbusinessangels.com

Provence Business Angels
Location: Marseille
Bio: Digital-related services, internet, mobile & software, health & medtech, cleantech
Investment: 50 - 500k
Business Type/Stage: Seed
Website: www.provenceangels.com
Contact email: contact@provenceangels.com

Reseau Capital
Location: Montreal
Website: www.reseaucapital.com
Contact email: inforeseau@reseaucapital.com

Saskatchewan Capital Network
Location: Saskatchewan
Website: www.saskcapitalnetwork.com

Startupxplore
Location: Valencia
Website: www.startupxplore.com
Contact email: info@startupxplore.com

Swiss ICT Investor Club (SICTIC)
Location: Zurich and Lausanne (Switzerland)
Currency: CHF
Bio: Business Angel club that invests in technology driven start-ups with a primary focus on those with domicile in Switzerland.
Investment: 200k - 1.5m
Website: www.sictic.ch
Contact email: info@sictic.ch

PART THREE

DOWN THE ROAD

3.1

WHAT TO DO WHEN YOU DON'T GET FUNDING

David Bateman and Jonathan Reuvid

Failure to attract funding will be a blow to self-confidence but is not necessarily the end of the road in your search for investment. Digest the disappointment then analyse objectively and in detail what went wrong and at what stage the project stalled. In this chapter we draw attention to the common causes for lack of traction and deal breakers and discuss remedial action.

FALLING AT THE FIRST FENCE

You selected a list of potential investors who appeared most suitable, emailed your concise Business Plan to them and followed up by telephone a week later where there was no reply. There was no favourable response. It is clear that your Business Plan did not attract more than a cursory glance. If the Plan followed the structure and format recommended in the earlier chapter the fault lies in the content and you should revisit and review in turn each of the pages submitted.

As a start, if you have not already done so, carry out a SWOT analysis of the overall theme and direction of your business strategy or revisit the previous analysis you made when drafting the Plan. Often displayed as a 2x2 matrix, there are four elements in a SWOT analysis:

- Strengths: characteristics of the business that give it an advantage over others;
- Weaknesses: characteristics of the business that place it at a disadvantage relative to others;
- Opportunities: elements in the environment that the business could exploit to its advantage;
- Threats: elements in the environment that could cause trouble for the business.

The questions for you now are:

- Have you overvalued the strengths or under-estimated the weaknesses of your business case?
- Are the advantages on which you have based your case sufficient to give it a genuinely unique selling point (USP)?
- Are there threats to growth and profitable development of the business sector you inhabit?
- Are new entrants to your niche market likely to enhance competition or threaten price structures?

If the answer to any of these questions is 'Yes' review and redraft the relevant sections, being sure to address each point with the positive action your business is taking. If all the answers are in the affirmative and clearly evident, you may not have a business case and should question whether there is a sound opportunity for your business. Finally, the most important question of all:

Does it make money and, if so, enough for an investor?

If you structured your Business Plan or included data other than recommended in Chapter One, try recasting it in that format before recirculating. Second opinions are always worth having and there are two sources that you can consult before a second round of emails. The first port of call is anyone to whom you have direct access or by referral who has been through the fundraising process and succeeded. The second could be one or more of the venture capital arms of university innovation spin-offs, such as Cambridge, Warwick or Manchester or one of the investment networks such as Oxford Investment Opportunity Network (OION). Any of these should be open to a telephone call after reading your revised Plan. Listen to what they say and amend the Business Plan accordingly.

FACE-TO-FACE ENCOUNTERS

If your first or second circulation of the Business Plan by email with telephone follow-up is successful in generating one or more invitations to meet, start preparing for first discussions. If there is still no interest after your second round, scan forward to the last section of this chapter.

First encounters are an opportunity to add colour to your written submission, to project your personality and to establish mutual respect and chemistry with investor management. There are some do's and don'ts to take into account as you prepare.

- Take at least one, but no more than two, members of your core management team with you. The investor is likely to field two or three members of its team. You need someone also to observe and read reactions to what you say and to keep notes. If you already have a financial director, they should be with you to answer questions that are put on the numbers. Moreover, you want to show that your company is not a "one man band".

- Keep your opening presentation firmly grounded on the information you have already sent. There is no need to say more about the financials at this point (if they were unacceptable, you wouldn't be there). Add more detail to the background and progress to date focusing on the USP that makes your business special and differentiates it from others in the same sector.

- Limit your opening remarks to no more than 15 minutes, though 10 minutes is better. (In the case of OION, investment candidates are schooled to keep strictly within 10 minutes referencing screenshots of selected pages from their Business Plans before pitching to investors in open session.)

- Decide in advance who is going to answer questions on each aspect of the Plan. For example, if the third member of your team is

responsible for marketing and sales they should give first replies on questions concerning the market, route to market and competition.
- Rehearse in advance, in particular your opening presentation which should be delivered fluently without hesitation and notes. Keep the tone informal without appearing casual or over-confident. Rehearse also answers to likely questions on the Plan which should be direct and without waffle.
- You will have the opportunity to ask questions of the investor towards the end of the meeting. Think in advance what you might like to ask but leave room to probe further on matters that arise in discussion.
- Debrief immediately following the meeting while your recollections are fresh.

If the meeting is successful, the investor may indicate that it would like to meet again, probably to clarify the business model and the granular detail behind the financials before considering what offer of funding can be made.

Alternatively, they may defer arrangements for a second encounter until they have discussed internally. Only if the discussion was totally negative is a rejection likely on the spot. If the decision is made afterwards not to pursue your proposal further, you will be able to ask for the reasons –and should do so.

Your debriefing will give insight on the elements of your Business Plan that were unsatisfactory and did not survive scrutiny. You will have the opportunity to address weaknesses before your next investor encounter. If there were no particular turn-offs in the Plan itself it may be simply that you failed to impress personally and there is little that you can do about that. In any case, ask the investor for feedback.

ENCOUNTERS OF THE SECOND KIND

At the next meeting the focus will be on probing the areas of greatest concern, further scrutiny of the business model and details of the financials. For start-ups where there is little or no financial history you should expect a granular examination of the detailed elements of all profit and loss and cashflow projections. If the investor is dissatisfied with the quality of the projections you should expect that any offer to invest will include the requirement to appoint a Non-Executive Director mandated to monitor the company's accounting function.

Another hurdle for start-ups is to convince that progress to date includes solid proof of concept. This may be difficult if the company has only recently started to trade and you are relying on market research which includes acceptance only of the concept and the product or service offering by potential customers without commitment to firm orders. Conversely, concerns about scalability may be harder to resolve for established companies with track records of less than stellar growth.

At this second meeting in your offices, there will be an opportunity for the investor to tour the facility and to meet the rest of your management team and staff. You should also prepare in advance of this meeting a more detailed analysis of the competition in your sector including top line financial data for any leading competitors who may be listed. Your objective this time is to answer all questions and provide additional information sufficient for the investor to confirm interest and to come back, either in writing or at a third meeting, with the basic terms of an investment offer.

Again, after this second encounter, carry out an immediate debriefing of the visit with all those who were party to any discussion.

THE INVESTMENT OFFER

Hopefully, the investor is now fully briefed and has completed a thorough investment sufficient to refer a proposal to its investment committee which will meet regularly. The outcome of this review may be approval for an offer to be made, a request that its investment team probes further and refers back for a decision or an outright decision to withdraw.

In the event that approval is given, the investor team will either call a new meeting to put forward an outline proposal for discussion and negotiation or issue a Term Sheet, subject to contract. In either case, having expressed your thanks, take your time to consider the terms before replying. A Term Sheet carries the implication that there may be little scope for negotiation.

This is the point where it is absolutely your responsibility to understand what you are being asked to agree to and you should involve your advisers, an external financial adviser if you have one, or an experienced corporate lawyer. As explained in the last chapter, packages of structured finance require careful assessment by a professional who can advise on the likely small print implications of each financial instrument. Negotiations should be completed as far as possible before acceptance of the Term Sheet which will be the starting-gun for preparing contracts. Haggling over basic terms of a contract once drafted is an expensive business for legal fees and can introduce an unnecessary sour note to relationships.

If no offer is forthcoming, once again you should seek clarity as to reasoning, before moving on to the next investor. In the event of a failure to agree terms, use this experience when engaging with the next potential investor.

ALTERNATIVES TO INVESTOR FUNDING

So, you've given it your best shot but failed to find an investor. Along the way you've acquired insight as to how investors think and, at the same time, exposed weaknesses in your project which may be irremediable until the business has travelled further.

As a start-up, if you still have confidence in the concept and how to deliver it, you may seek a grant of up to £20,000 from the Small Business Research Initiative by application for a SMART grant from Innovate UK provided that you can self-fund at least 30% of the cost. The money can be used for market research but not for sales.

If your business is more advanced in its R&D activities you may apply for 70% of the cost of technical feasibility studies and industrial research up to £100,000 and up to £1 million for a development stage project. Other grants are available under the Catalyst programmes run jointly by Innovate UK and the Research Councils for specific sectors such as biomedical, agri-tech and energy. Similar EU grants for UK SMEs from the EUREKA Eurostars programme may not be available after Brexit.

Aside from the banks, there are now also new sources of lending available, such as through new lenders such as Funding Circle, who will lend to new businesses based on their own criteria with much faster decision times (usually 24-72 hours). Loans through these new lenders are usually anywhere from a month for short-term need through to up to five years. It is important to confirm the interest rate, and whether there are any early repayment charges so you can repay the loans in full once revenues increase and you have the cash available.

Additionally, crowdfunding has become an increasingly popular alternative route to raise finance. This usually means giving equity away in small chunks to a large number of people via an online platform in return for capital, and often gifts such as free products and other offers. Crowdfunding has proved successful for a large number of companies, though it usually favours those with an existing large social media or customer following that they can promote the offer to.

By going back to the drawing board you may be able to restructure your Plan to more modest growth targets over a longer period of time involving fewer resources and requiring less working capital. You may have to fund this reduced plan in the medium term using your own money and perhaps with support from family and friends. Using your personal assets as security for bank borrowing may be an unacceptable risk and that decision is your call alone. Tomorrow may be another day for investor funding.

3.2

END GAME

David Bateman

Think about why you are writing a Business Plan. It's to get investment, right? And in order for you to succeed here, it means that an investor has to recover their original investment plus a decent return. The mechanism by which the investor achieves this is typically through a process called the 'exit' and this is how the investor extracts their original capital from your business and makes a profit in the process. Moreover, the 'exit' is usually the way that an entrepreneur makes money from their business – and often a successful exit can mean some big numbers, reaching into the millions sometimes. The exit is the final piece of the jigsaw that an investor must get comfortable with, and so I tend to call this last stage the 'end game'.

Let's not forget that the reason the investor invests in the first place is to make money from your business. They are not investing money as a loan, from which they may make a modest return on their investment, and they are not investing on a charitable basis, just because they like you. An investor puts money in your business to make more money: it's as simple as that. If this all sounds a little too brutally capitalist, then you need to think twice about asking for an investment in the first place, as making money is the name of the game here. In order to achieve this, the investor must, at some point, be able to get their hands on the cash – and this is where the exit, or 'end game', comes into play.

I am often surprised by the number of Business Plans that fail to mention the exit. After all, the plan must be more about the investor's needs than your own, given you are trying to persuade them to put their hard-earned money into your venture. By providing some clarity on the question of the exit in your Business Plan, you are catering to the investor's needs.

When I see no reference to an exit in a Business Plan, it usually rings alarm bells. It says to me that the entrepreneur or business owner is not thinking things through all the way to the end game. This can be dangerous because it suggests a lack of clear goals. So, make sure that you include this page in your plan: it is an easy win. It shows that you are 'worldly wise' as a business operator, and clearly demonstrates that you understand what an investor ultimately requires.

Exit Mechanisms

There are many mechanisms that offer a potential route to exit, but the three most typical and relevant here are:

1. Sale
2. Public listing (also known as an 'IPO')
3. Profit distributions and/or debt repayment

Let's take a look at what each of these means.

1. Sale

This is simply where you sell your business to another business. The general activity of businesses acquiring other businesses is often referred to as 'M&A', which means 'Mergers and Acquisitions'. When a sale successfully goes through, the proceeds are split between the shareholders of the business that has been bought, on a basis that is proportionate to their ownership. Ideally, the amount that the original investor receives from the sale will be far greater than the amount they invested at the outset.

Typically, there are two types of sale that take place. One is known as a 'trade sale'. This means that the business that is buying your (usually much smaller) company is often operating in the same sector, or 'trade'. The other type of sale is made by a professional investor – typically private equity. Private equity businesses pool together large amounts of money and then aim to buy smaller businesses to then improve or consolidate them with similar businesses in order to create more value. The private equity buyer will then aim to exit the business themselves at a later date, through a trade sale, another private equity business or a public listing.

2. Public listing

This is also known as an IPO (initial public offering), or 'flotation', and was all the rage during the dotcom boom. Rather than selling your shares to another business, you make your shares available for purchase by the 'public' via a stock exchange where they are freely tradable. In reality, although it is called a 'public offering', it is usually large investment institutions such as pension funds and insurance companies that make up the bulk of the buyers of your shares, rather than members of the general public. The price at which your shares are initially made available on the stock exchange will be much higher than the valuation at which the investor originally acquired them. At that point the business would have been far less profitable and much more risky – so now the investor is rewarded for sharing some of this risk.

However, IPOs are increasingly difficult and becoming a less attractive option to an entrepreneur. The listing process is expensive and because the world's stock markets are so large now, your business must have significant critical mass in order for an IPO to be a valid option. Indeed, when there is an IPO of a new business, it will often have private equity investors as full owners, or at least part owners, alongside the original founding team.

3. Profit distribution and/or loan repayment

It might be the case that neither a trade sale nor a flotation takes place. Perhaps there is not an interested buyer or perhaps you are simply not big enough to float. Indeed this is often a common scenario for many businesses.

However, as the business continues to grow and become more profitable, an investor can be paid back gradually, making a return through the profits generated. When payments are made to the shareholders of a business from the profits in this way, they are called dividend payments. This is a valuable mechanism, as it means an investor can recover their initial investment over time while retaining the additional benefit of a potential trade sale or flotation in the future. Sometimes an original investment might be made as a loan, but such a deal would also include some shares in the business (often referred to as 'equity upside' or an 'equity kicker'). The business repays the loan over time, which returns the original amount invested back to the investor, and then the investor is free to enjoy any future dividends safe in the knowledge that the investment is now risk-free.

This type of end game may indeed be very appealing for certain types of investors, if a sale or listing is not an option. It can provide a recurring stream of dividends that pays out on an annual basis and demonstrates that their investment is not lost. Typically, this would suit the less institutional end of the investment community such as angel investors, or friends and family. Conversely, a private equity firm will always be looking for a more aggressive and complete exit, such as a sale. The reason for this is that a private equity firm tends to operate on a three to seven year time horizon in order to get all of their investment back, along with a very significant return, that is expected to be many multiples of that original amount.

It might be difficult to be clear which option is the most likely in the early stages of your business, and it may be some time before it is apparent which is the most viable mechanism for exit. Despite this, rather than simply listing the three options above in your plan, you will need to justify why you think any of them might represent a viable option.

COMPARABLES

The best way to justify a potential exit strategy is to refer to what has happened in the past with similar companies in similar sectors, as well as making reference to what the current trend is. For example, if several companies have undergone trade sales in your sector in recent years, I suggest that this should be your identified aim as an exit. In the late 1990s, technology companies generally sought public listings as their preferred exit route, and public stock markets saw a dotcom feeding frenzy as a result. At that time, a public listing might well have been a realistic exit mechanism to aim for.

Things have moved on since then, and although investors generally recognise the Internet and technology sectors as having huge potential and as established markets now, some lessons have been learned. Consequently, you see far fewer technology listings than in the heyday of the dotcom boom and, now, it is typically the larger, better-established firms that seek an IPO. As a result, many smaller, fast-growing technology firms tend to seek an exit through a trade sale to these larger, publicly listed businesses.

In the current economic environment at the time of writing, I would suggest that specifying a trade sale as your intended exit makes the most sense as an initial aim, assuming there are examples of this in your sector already – though if your business is a world-beater, you may feel that you want to go for a public listing, where fortunes can be made (and lost!). If that's the case, and your ambitions know no bounds, then specify an IPO as your form of exit – but make sure you can justify this with examples of recent flotations of similar businesses in similar sectors.

When outlining your exit, you should where possible clearly demonstrate similar exits of comparable companies. These are known as 'comparables'. It is important to include reference to comparables, as they show the investor that there is indeed a mechanism in your business sector by which they can crystallise a return on their investment in cold, hard cash.

For example, let's say that I want to start an Internet comparison website that focuses on financial products and services. The site will compare and contrast the best prices for insurance products, savings accounts, pension funds, and so on. On this page of your Plan you should show a list of comparable businesses that have successfully exited. Be clear about what the exit values and multiples were ('multiples' meaning how many times bigger the exit value was than profits or sales generated for that year). For example:

- moneysupermarket.com floated 2009. Current valuation £600m. Multiple 12x EBITDA.
- beatthatquote.com trade sale to Google for £38m. Multiple 10x revenue.

In these examples I have shown only exits in the UK, but it is perfectly acceptable, and advisable, to include comparable exits internationally.

At the inception of moneysupermarket.com, someone almost certainly invested just a few hundred thousand pounds for a meaningful stake in the business. Imagine that you invested £100K for 10 per cent when the business started out. Your £100K would now be worth £60 million! That's the power of an exit. Comparable exits will reassure investors that they are not entering into a wild goose chase, and also help justify the valuation you place on your business when asking for investment. It is a bit like the 'proof of concept' for your product or service, except in this case it is more a 'proof of exit', whereby you show that successful exits in your space have been achieved.

If there are no comparable exits – which may be the case if you are a genuine first-mover – then be honest and make that clear. But beware, this is very rare and, if you cannot find a valuation for your competition, it often means that you are not looking hard enough. However, a lack of comparables is not necessarily a completely bad thing and may indeed be seen as a potential opportunity, in that you might be the first in your sector to sell or float.

When highlighting a sale as your most likely exit, it is essential to list those companies that are likely to acquire your business, especially if they have been acquisitive in the past. Try to be realistic about which companies you name here. If you are a technology company, don't just list the obvious suspects such as Google or Facebook: do your homework on which companies are the big players in the same or similar sectors in which you operate, and which of them might want to gain access to your particular space through acquisition rather than developing a similar product or service themselves. Talk to industry specialists who understand the landscape, and try to acquire a feel for what might make sense.

If you feel that profit distributions are the most appropriate mechanism by which investors will make a return, make sure that these payments fit with the projected profits and timeframe in your profit-and-loss statements. This may sound obvious, but it is all too easy to be over-optimistic and create a mismatch between projected profits and projected investor payouts. You should state in your plan the anticipated timeframe in which you intend to make these dividend payments so that the investor has a clear indication as to when they get their money back and start making a return on the investment.

CONCLUSION

Finally, outlining an exit, even if it is a long way off, makes a fitting conclusion to your Business Plan. Just as an exit is the logical ending for your business, so it is also for your Plan. Remember that the purpose of your Plan is to tell the story of your business so that the investor gets the whole picture as clearly as possible. Just as a story needs a clear ending, so does your Plan.